The Oresteia

Publication of this book has been made possible, in part, through support from the Anonymous Fund of the College of Letters and Science at the University of Wisconsin–Madison and the generous support and enduring vision of Warren G. Moon.

The Oresteia

Agamemnon, Libation Bearers, and *The Holy Goddesses*

AESCHYLUS

A verse translation by
David Mulroy,
with introduction and notes

The University of Wisconsin Press

The University of Wisconsin Press
1930 Monroe Street, 3rd Floor
Madison, Wisconsin 53711-2059
uwpress.wisc.edu

3 Henrietta Street, Covent Garden
London WC2E 8LU, United Kingdom
eurospanbookstore.com

Printed in the United States of America

This book may be available in a digital edition.

Library of Congress Cataloging-in-Publication Data
Names: Aeschylus, author. | Mulroy, David D., 1943– translator, writer of
supplementary textual content. | Container of (expression): Aeschylus.
Agamemnon. English. | Container of (expression): Aeschylus. Choephori.
English. | Container of (expression): Aeschylus. Eumenides. English.
Title: The Oresteia: agamemnon, libation bearers, and the holy goddesses / a
verse translation by David Mulroy, with introduction and notes.
Other titles: Oresteia. English | Wisconsin studies in classics.
Description: Madison, Wisconsin : The University of Wisconsin Press, [2018]
| Series: Wisconsin studies in classics
| Includes bibliographical references and index.
Identifiers: LCCN 2017044983| ISBN 9780299315603 (cloth: alk. paper)
| ISBN 9780299315641 (pbk.)
Subjects: LCSH: Aeschylus—Translations into English. | Agamemnon, King of
Mycenae (Mythological character)—Drama. | Orestes, King of Argos
(Mythological character)—Drama. | Electra (Greek mythological
figure)—Drama. | LCGFT: Tragedies (Drama)
Classification: LCC PA3827.A7 M77 2018 | DDC 882/.01—dc23
LC record available at https://lccn.loc.gov/2017044983

For

Richard W. Johnston

Contents

Preface

This volume contains my translations of the three plays constituting Aeschylus' *Oresteia*: *Agamemnon*, *Libation Bearers*, and *Eumenides*. The University of Wisconsin Press published *Agamemnon* separately in 2016 since that play is often read and taught independently, in world literature classes, for example, as an example of the best of classical Greek tragedy. Yet *Libation Bearers* and *Eumenides* are not devoid of interest—far from it.

Read by itself, *Agamemnon* is about individuals struggling in vain to escape the consequences of their evil acts. In *Libation Bearers* and *Eumenides*, Aeschylus widens his view and strikes a hopeful note. Athens, personified by the goddess Athena, replaces Orestes as the real hero. Aeschylus implies that the democratic city-state alone has mastered the tools needed to resolve the conflicts that arise where ties of blood are all that count: persuasion instead of compulsion; disinterested reasoning instead of blind loyalties. The theme is nothing if not timely.

I have recently been won over to the view that the third play of the trilogy should be called *The Holy Goddesses* or *The Furies*, not *Eumenides* (see appendix 5), although I employ *Eumenides* as the title in my discussion of other aspects of the trilogy to avoid confusion.

Two items in my lists of characters may confuse some readers. First, *Coryphaeus*. This is just an ancient Greek word meaning "head" in the sense of "chief" or "leader." In the context of

Greek tragedy, it denotes the leader of the chorus, who shared its attributes. He played an old soldier in *Agamemnon*, an elderly slave woman in *Libation Bearers*, and a Fury in *Eumenides*, but he had an additional function. Besides singing and dancing, he could and did converse with the actors.

Second, despite what you may have seen in other translations (including my *Agamemnon*), the correct spelling of Mrs. Agamemnon's name is *Clytaemestra* (Κλυταιμήστρα), not *Clytemnestra*. The former spelling is found in the most ancient evidence, such as inscriptions on Athenian pottery. The *n* is thought to have been introduced by Byzantine scholars on the mistaken assumption that her name was a play on the verb *mnaomai* ("to court" or "woo"). The other root involved in the name's supposed etymology was *klyto-* ("famous" or—in Clytaemestra's case—"infamous").[1]

In preparing this translation, I relied chiefly on Alan Sommerstein's Loeb Library *Oresteia* for help in resolving textual and interpretive issues. In addition, I regularly consulted Taplin's *Stagecraft of Aeschylus*, Raeburn and Thomas's commentary on *Agamemnon*, Garvie's commentary on *Choephori*, and Podlecki's on *Eumenides*. All translations are mine.

Note

1. Cf. Alan H. Sommerstein, *Aeschylus, "Oresteia,"* x n4; Eduard Fraenkel, ed., *Aeschylus: "Agamemnon,"* commentary on line 84.

Introduction

I maintain that Aeschylus—and not, as some say,
Euripides—first introduced the spectacle of
drunken characters in tragedy. In the *Cabiri*[1] he
depicts Jason's comrades drunk. In other words,
he attributes to his heroes what he himself did as
a tragic dramatist: he composed his tragedies
while drunk.

ATHENAEUS 10.428

At the great annual springtime festival of Dionysus in ancient
Athens, three tragic poets competed against each other. Each
presented a set of three original tragedies and a farcical satyr play.
First performed in the spring of 458 BCE, Aeschylus' *Oresteia*
won the first prize then. It has the distinction now of being
the only complete dramatic trilogy to have been preserved. Its
three tragedies are entitled *Agamemnon*, *Libation Bearers*, and
Eumenides.

    The *Oresteia* tells the story of Orestes. He is the son of King
Agamemnon, the leader of the Greeks' attack on Troy. When
Agamemnon returns from the war, he is murdered by his faith-
less wife, Clytaemestra. Through his oracle, the god Apollo tells
Orestes that he must avenge his father by killing his mother
and her lover. Having done so, the youth is pursued by the

Furies, horrible underworld goddesses who punish those who murder blood relatives. He flees to Athens, where the goddess Athena establishes a court that tries Orestes and finds him guiltless. She placates the Furies, who become benevolent goddesses dwelling under the ground in Athens.

The friendship between Athena and the Furies stands for the reconciliation of two religious dispensations that competed for influence in classical Athens. The more primitive rites focused on the spirits of the dead and the need to win and keep their good will. Generations of the living and the dead were bound to each other through the indissoluble ties of blood. Sons were punished for the sins of their fathers.

The worship of Zeus and the other Olympians was infused with a different spirit. Their rituals celebrated the good things of life, including song and dance, and were intertwined with the government of the polis, which made the good life possible. A person's service to the city was more important than the identity of his ancestors. Through the taming of the Furies, the *Oresteia* suggests that ties of blood should play an important but subordinate role in the life of an enlightened community. Its disagreements should be resolved through rational discourse, not blind loyalties. This theme gains in relevance when one reflects that the modern equivalents of blood ties are race and ethnicity.

My approach to translation is distinguished by the lengths I go to in order to recreate the formalism of Greek tragedy through regular meters and some end rhyme. One inevitably hears the criticism that such an approach necessarily sounds repetitive and monotonous. Of course, I disagree. I have written elsewhere that my translations ought to be read aloud, but that is not likely to happen and would not guarantee a fair hearing anyway. A better request is for readers to imagine, as they read, how the lines would sound when performed by a Method actor. When that is done, it becomes obvious that the variations of natural speech easily overwhelm regular meters and even end rhyme. In natural speech, stressed syllables are not all stressed alike. Some stresses are heavy, some are light to the point of vanishing, others fall somewhere in between. Moreover, natural speakers constantly change their tempo, volume, and affect. They shout, whisper, pause, laugh, weep, interrogate, insinuate, and so on. Beneath this cascade of natural variations, the use of a regular meter or a system of end rhymes is scarcely noticeable. They do have an important function, however. They subject the otherwise chaotic flow of words to a perceptible degree of orderliness and forward momentum. End rhymes require their own kind of variety. Words that rhyme should be as different as possible in grammar, meaning, and shape. As is often the case in the realm of aesthetics, the pleasant effect of strict meters and end rhymes is created not by sameness but by a tension between opposites. Monotony is one pole, chaos the other. The pleasing effects are in the middle.

Appreciation of the *Oresteia* also requires recognition of its transgressive character. There are a number of passages in which the normal rules of logic or propriety are kicked in the mud, as Aeschylus would have said. Scholarly commentators tend to interpret such passages in ways that restore their rationality and dignity, but viewed collectively they seem to be parts of a deliberate pattern. Dramatists inevitably project their own character through their work. Thus we have the elegant Sophocles, the irreverent Euripides, and—as Athenaeus noted—the drunken Aeschylus. His characters sometimes become obviously irrational as when Electra infers from a footprint identical to her own that Orestes has returned (*Libation Bearers* 208–211) or when Clytaemestra tells Cassandra to wave her hand if she doesn't understand speech (*Agamemnon* 1061). There are passages of highly questionable taste, as when Aeschylus has Clytaemestra use an obscenity (*histotribēs*, mast-rubber) as part of her crudely sexual vaunting over Cassandra's body (*Agamemnon* 1440–1447) and later bare her breast when begging her son for mercy (*Libation Bearers* 896–898). When it pleases him Aeschylus is indifferent to familiar facts. He has Apollo and Orestes both refer to the easy two- or three-day journey by foot from Delphi to Athens as an epic trek over land and sea (*Eumenides* 74–80 and 235–243). Again, Apollo and Orestes both say that Orestes was cleansed of guilt by a shower of piglets' blood at Delphi (*Eumenides* 281–283 and 576–578) even though Orestes' visit to Delphi is dramatized without any such ritual taking place (*Eumenides* 85–93). Other passages seem to have come from an intoxicated mind just by virtue of their strangeness. One thinks of Apollo's terrified priestess scurrying out of her Fury-infested temple on hands and knees (*Eumenides* 36–39) or of Orestes having a team of attendants unroll and display the gigantic robe in which Clytaemestra slew Agamemnon (*Libation Bearers* 983–990) as if it were a horrible weapon.

I do not mean to imply that Aeschylus was a drunkard in real life. The impression that one has of an author on the basis of a text and the author's real character may be quite different. I do think that Aeschylus' wild authorial persona contributes significantly to the pleasure of reading or hearing his plays. It contrasts nicely with the rigid conventions of the Greek stage.

Other matters are worthy of inclusion in an introduction to a work as rich as the *Oresteia*, but many readers, I'm sure, would prefer to proceed at once to reading the play. I have therefore followed a friend's suggestion and recast other material as a series of appendixes printed after the translation, with the clear implication that reading them is optional:

1. Synopses: A quick summary of each of the three tragedies.
2. Aeschylus' Biography: Despite his great contributions to Greek literature, Aeschylus wished to be remembered as a soldier rather than as a poet—or so we're told.

3. The *Oresteia* and Myth: The *Oresteia* is the culmination of the cycle of myths beginning with the story of the famous sinner Tantalus.

4. The *Oresteia* and Politics: The trilogy was arguably an expression of support for the policies of Ephialtes and Pericles, champions of the party of the people.

5. Renaming *Eumenides*: I endorse Sommerstein's opinion that the third play of the *Oresteia* should be called *The Holy Goddesses*, or possibly *The Furies*.

6. Metrical Terms and Practices: What you need to know about strophes and antistrophes and other metrical terms to appreciate Aeschylus' art.

7. The Greek Stage: The appearance of the stage, exits and entrances, special effects.

Note

1. The title of a lost play by Aeschylus. The Cabiri were minor deities, sons of Hephaestus, worshipped on the island of Lemnos, the first stop in the travels of Jason and the Argonauts.

Pronunciation Guide and Glossary of Proper Names

Key

ə: as in the first and last syllable of *America*
a: as in *bat*
ä: as in *father*
ā: as in *say*
e: as in *get*
ē: as in *be*
i: as in *it*
ī: as in *eye*
ō: as in *go*
ȯ: as in *awe*
ü: as in *loose*

Achaea (ə-kē´-ə): another name for Greece; adj. Achaean (ə-kē´-ən).
Aegisthus (i-jis´-thəs): Clytaemestra's lover.
Agamemnon (a-gə-mem´-nän): king of Argos, conqueror of Troy.
Alexander (a-lig-zan´-dər): another name for Paris, prince of Troy.

Amazons (a′-mə-zäns): legendary women warriors who invaded Athens during the reign of Theseus.

Apollo (ə-pä′-lō): god of prophecy, worshipped at Delphi.

Areopagus (ar-ē-ä′-pə-gəs): rocky plateau near the Acropolis, meeting place of an ancient council.

Ares (ar′-ēz): god of war.

Argos (är′-gōs): city and region of southeastern Peloponnesus; adj. Argive (är′-gīv).

Artemis (är′-tə-məs): virgin huntress goddess.

Athena (ə-thē′-nə): daughter of Zeus, renowned for wisdom.

Atreus (ā′-trē-əs): king of Argos, father of Agamemnon and Menelaus; adj. Atreid (ā′-trē-id).

Calchas (kal′-kəs): Greek army's prophet.

Cassandra (kə-san′-drə): Priam's daughter, priestess of Apollo.

Cilissa (si-li′-sə): Orestes' old nurse.

Clytaemestra (klī-tə-mes′-trə): Agamemnon's wife, queen of Argos.

Danaans (dan′-i-əns): another name for the Greeks.

Delos (dē′-lȯs): a very small Aegean island, Apollo's birthplace.

Delphi (del′-fī): site of Apollo's oracular temple.

Electra (ē-lek′-trə): Orestes' sister.

Erinys (i-ri′-nəs): a Fury; plural Erinyes (i-ri′-nē-ēz).

Euboea (yü-bē′-ə): large island stretching along the coast of eastern Greece.

Gorgons (gȯr′-gənz): three monstrous sisters whose look turned men to stone.

Hades (hā′-dēz): god of the underworld.

Helen (he′-lən): Menelaus' wife, who eloped with Paris.

Helios (hē′-lē-əs): god of the sun.

Hellas (he′-läs): Greece; adj. Hellene (hel′-lēn).

Hephaestus (hi-fe′-stəs): god of the blacksmith's forge and fire.

Hermes (hər′-mēz): messenger god, guide of dead souls to the underworld.

Ida (ī'-də): mountain in the vicinity of Troy.

Ilium (i'-lē-əm:) another name for Troy.

Iphigenia (if-ə-jə-nī'-ä): Agamemnon and Clytaemestra's daughter.

Ixion (ik-sī'-ən): king punished for trying to seduce Hera.

Lemnos (lem'-näs): a large Aegean island west of Troy; adj. Lemnian (lem'-nē-ən).

Loxias (läx'-ē-əs): another name for Apollo.

Menelaus (me-nə-lā'-əs): Agamemnon's brother, Helen's husband.

Orestes (ə-res'-tēz): Agamemnon and Clytaemestra's son.

Paean (pē'-ən): healing god sometimes identified with Apollo; paean: a joyous hymn.

Pallas (pa'-ləs): another name for Athena.

Pan (pan): shepherds' god.

Paris (par'-əs): prince of Troy, Helen's lover.

Parnassus (pär-na'-səs): a mountain in central Greece, the location of the oracle of Delphi; adj. Parnassian (pär-na'-sē-ən).

Phocis (fō'-kəs): district in central Greece including Delphi; adj. Phocian (fō'-shin).

Pleisthenes (plīs'-the-nēz): according to some, the real father of Agamemnon and Menelaus; adj. Pleisthenid (plīs'-the-nid).

Priam (prī'-əm): king of Troy; adj. Priamid (prē'-ə-mid).

Pylades (pi'-lə-dēz): Orestes' friend and constant companion.

Pytho (pī'-thō): another name for Delphi.

Scamander (skə-man'-dər): river in the vicinity of Troy.

Strophius (strō'-fē-əs): father of Orestes' companion Pylades.

Theseus (thē'-sē-əs): heroic king of Athens.

Thrace (thrās): barbarian land north of Greece; adj. Thracian (thrā'-shən).

Thyestes (thī-es'-tēz): brother of Atreus, father of Aegisthus.

Troy (troi): Priam's royal city; adj. Trojan (trō-jən).

Zeus (züs): king of the gods.

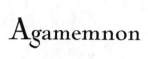

Agamemnon

Characters

WATCHMAN, a slave of Agamemnon
CHORUS, twelve elderly citizens of Argos
CORYPHAEUS, the leader of the chorus
CLYTAEMESTRA, Agamemnon's wife, queen of Argos
HERALD, a messenger in Agamemnon's army
AGAMEMNON, king of Argos, leader of the expedition against
    Troy
CASSANDRA, daughter of Priam, king of Troy, now Agamem-
    non's captive
CLYTAEMESTRA'S ATTENDANTS
AEGISTHUS, Agamemnon's cousin, Clytaemestra's lover
SOLDIERS, Aegisthus' bodyguard
CAPTAIN OF THE GUARDS, officer in charge of Aegisthus'
    bodyguard

(The play is set in Argos before the palace of King
Agamemnon. The WATCHMAN, who speaks the opening
lines, is stationed on the palace's roof. CLYTAEMESTRA
will enter from the skēnē, which represents the palace,
via a central door.)

WATCHMAN:
I ask the gods to end this yearlong watch
on Agamemnon's roof, where I support

my chin on forepaws like a dog and watch
the starry congregations night by night,
the ether's brilliant dynasties that bring
wintery chill and summer heat to men.
I watch their constellations rise and sink,
hoping to see a signal torch ignite,
a flash of fire bringing word from Troy.
The word is "captured." Why such vigilance?   10
A woman's eager, manly heart's in charge.
Therefore I keep a restless, dew-damp bed,
which dreams have never looked upon, since fear
forever hovers—fear instead of sleep.
My eyelids never stay together long,
and when I sing or whistle melodies
to drug my sleepless mind, I end the song
in tears for all this house's suffering,
this house once governed well, no longer so.
But let my labors have a happy end   20
and that auspicious light relieve this gloom!

      (After a pause, a flame appears in the distance.)

Hello! My beacon! Bringing light of day
and dancing choruses to Greece
to celebrate the fortune you announce!
Eeoo! Eeoo!
That shrill alarm's for Agamemnon's wife,
for she must quickly leave her bed and raise
a joyous cheer to celebrate this light,
if Ilium[1] has truly fallen now,
as this burnt message clearly signifies,   30
and I myself will dance a prelude first.

    1. Another name for Troy.

(He dances a jig.)

I'll use my masters' lucky cast somehow.
This vigil rolled a triple six for me.
Just let me see the house's lord return
and let me hold his kindly hand in mine.
I'm silent otherwise. A giant ox
stands on my tongue. If palace walls could talk,
you'd hear some lively tales. Perhaps you catch
my drift. That's good. If not, . . . my memory fails.

(Exit WATCHMAN down the rear of the skēnē. Enter
the CHORUS via a parodos.)

CHORUS:
Ten years have elapsed since the great   Anapests (40-103)
Lord Menelaus,[2] the plaintiff,
accuser of Priam,[3] together
with Lord Agamemnon, the Atreids'[4]
powerful wagon of honor,
a dyad divinely endowed
with scepters and sovereign thrones,[5]
launched myriad ships from the land,
an Argive[6] attack expedition.

2. Agamemnon's brother. The Trojan War was fought to recover his
wife, Helen, from her Trojan lover, Paris.
3. The king of Troy, Paris's father.
4. The Atreids (sons of Atreus) are Agamemnon and Menelaus.
5. In Homer's *Iliad*, Agamemnon is the king of Mycenae, while Menelaus
rules Sparta by virtue of his marriage to Helen. Aeschylus depicts Agamemnon
as the king of Argos and leaves Menelaus' realm unspecified.
6. "Argive" means "from the city-state of Argos," but it is also used to
denote Greeks in general.

They angrily shouted for war,
like vultures who circle their nests,
who row through the air overcome
by unbearable pain as they view
the waste of the labor they spent on their young.
Above, some Apollo[7] or Pan[8]
or possibly Zeus[9] has detected
the shrill lamentation of birds,
his fellow sky-dwellers, and sends
a belated avenger to punish the crime.
Thus Zeus, whose superior might
protects the hospitable,[10] sends
the children that Atreus[11] sired
against Alexander[12] of Troy;
at stake—a promiscuous wife.
And many a bone-weary grapple
with knees driven down in the dirt
and the ritual breaking of spears
awaits both the Trojans and Greeks.
Things are as they are. Their completion is fixed.
Don't count on the burning of victims
or liquids untouched by the flame
to quench inexorable rage.
We ourselves were excluded from honor

7. God of prophecy.
8. Shepherds' god, the guardian of flocks.
9. King of the gods.
10. Zeus is frequently called Xenios, "the hospitable." One of his functions is to oversee the sacred relationship between hosts and those who stay in their homes as guests. Paris violated this relationship in the worst way by running away with his host's wife.
11. Father of Agamemnon and Menelaus.
12. Another name for Paris.

because of our elderly flesh.
The army rejected us. Now
we linger reduced to supporting
our infantile strength on our canes.
The marrow that throbs in a child
resembles an elderly man's,
for Ares[13] is absent in each.
When the foliage withers, old age
travels a three-footed path,
wandering weak as a child,
a dream that is seen by the day.
But you, Clytaemestra, our queen,
daughter Tyndareus[14] bred,
please tell us what's happening now
explaining the message you heard,
the new information for which
you circle the city with flame.
The altars of all of the gods,
of demons above and below,
of doorway and marketplace gods,
all of them blaze with your gifts.
From every direction, a fire
soars to the top of the sky,
induced by the gentle, untainted
persuasion of sacrosanct oil,
oil from the storeroom of kings.
Please tell us what's happening now,
revealing whatever you can,

13. Ares, god of war, personifies the furious rage of warriors in the heat of battle.

14. Tynadareus (tin-dar´-ē-əs), king of Sparta, father of Helen and Clytaemestra.

what custom permits you to say;
become the physician of care
that occasionally troubles our brain,
while comforting hopes that are raised
by the victims you joyously burn,
ward off the insatiable fear
and scatter the heartbreaking pain.

I'm authorized to sing about
    the powerful estate
of men in charge of leading us
    along the road of fate.

By grace divine the time that's passed
    since first I came along
grants my breath persuasion still,
    and that's the strength of song.

I sing of how a bird sign sped
    Achaea's[15] *double throne,*
two single-minded kings, to Troy,
    and they were not alone.

They led the Hellenes' blooming youth
    to Teucer's[16] *distant land,*
and each of them had fixed a spear
    in his avenging hand.

15. "Achaea" in a narrow sense denotes a region in the northwest Peloponnesus. Like "Argos," the term is also used, as here, to refer to Greece in general.

16. The Teucer (tü´-sər) referenced here is a mythological ancestor of the kings of Troy—not to be confused with the Greek Teucer, half-brother of the greater Ajax.

The navy's kings peruse the sky.
*   The kings of birds*[17] *appear,*
one black, the other white behind.
*   Eventually they near*

the palace roof beams on the right,
*   the hand that wields the spear.*
And now they're perching on the beams
*   where everything is clear.*

They're feasting on a pregnant hare
*   and eat her offspring too.*
She tripped before the finish line.
*   Her racing days are through.*

"Ah Linus,[18] *Linus!" shout, but good prevail!*

The army's prudent prophet[19] *sees*   Antistrophe I (122–139)
*   lord Atreus's sons,*
so differing in temperament,
*   and knows that they're the ones,*

the rabbit-eating warriors
*   who keep the men in line,*
and so he spoke these words aloud,
*   interpreting the sign.*

---

17. Eagles.

18. Linus (lī´-nəs), a tragic mythological musician of whom different stories were told (e.g., that he was a music teacher slain by the young Heracles). His name was invoked in songs of lamentation.

19. As in the *Iliad*, the army's prophet is a gifted seer named Calchas.

"In time this army shall obtain
     control of Priam's state.
A violent fate will overtake
     the herds outside his gate,

the cattle owned in common there,
     but let us not permit
the anger of divinities
     to stain the armored bit

we've forged for Troy ahead of time,
     for Artemis[20] abounds
in pity, and she's come to hate
     her father's wingéd hounds

because they cruelly sacrificed
     the poor defenseless hare,
together with the little ones
     that she was going to bear.

Their sorry fate arouses holy
     Artemis's zeal.
The patroness of childbirth, she
     detests the eagles' meal."

"Ah Linus, Linus!" shout, but good prevail!

"Kind though the lovely goddess is   Epode (140–159)

20. The virgin huntress, daughter of Zeus and sister of Apollo. She is also a goddess of childbirth and the protector of the young, animal and human alike.

to glaring lions' drops of dew
and all the young things nursed in fields,
    she'll make the signs come true,

signs promising success but flawed.
    Eeoo, good Paean![21] Hear my plea!
May she not fashion adverse winds
    that keep us off the sea,

long-lasting blasts that freeze the ships,
    because she wants another life,
a grim and lawless ritual,
    an architect of strife,

a rite not fearing any man.
    Beware! A cunning steward waits,
an Anger who'll avenge the child."
    Thus Calchas roared their fates.

He added many good things too,
    the royal houses' destiny,
inferred from birds along the road.
    Now sing in harmony:

"Ah Linus, Linus!" shout, but good prevail!

Zeus, whoever he may be,   Strophe 2 (160–166)
in case that title pleases him—
I call him by that name because
I cannot find a synonym,

---

21. An obscure healing god sometimes equated with Apollo or his son
Asclepius. Choral songs addressed to Apollo were also called paeans.

although I've weighed all other terms.
There's only Zeus if ever we
shall truly shed the useless weight
of our perplexity.

One great before was full of fight.[22]   Antistrophe 2 (167–175)
He might as well have never been.
The next contender met his match
and left dismayed. He couldn't win.
The men who celebrate the crowns
triumphant Zeus has won attain
the pinnacle of wisdom found
in any human brain.

Zeus, who started mortal man   Strophe 3 (176–183)
     down understanding's trail,
hid wisdom deep in suffering,
     no other routes avail.
Sleep disappears and in its stead
     the memory of pain
drips around the restless heart,
     a never-ending rain.
Self-knowledge comes to those who wish
     and those who wish it not.
Our helmsmen are divinities,
     and they're a violent lot.

Achaea's aging admiral   Antistrophe 3 (184–191)
     was not at all inclined

22. Here Aeschylus apparently refers to the Hesiodic myth (*Theogony* 154–210) that the first king of the gods, Uranus, was overthrown by Cronus and that the latter was overthrown by Zeus.

to disregard a prophecy.
  It never left his mind.
He wavered in the changing blasts
  of fortune, well aware
that hostile winds that froze the ships
  were hard for men to bear—
men stranded there in Aulis,[23] *where*
  tide waters ebb and flow,
across the straits from Chalcis[24] *with*
  provisions running low.

Paralyzing winds from Thrace[25]   Strophe 4 (192–204)
  had come with hunger, bad
anchorage, and rotten ropes,
  and sailors driven mad,
long-lasting winds that tore apart
  Greek blossoms by the sea,
but when the prophet barked aloud
  a graver remedy,[26]
a way to end the bitter storm,
  it stunned the foremost men.
Their royal scepters banged the ground,
  and tears fell freely then.

23. Aulis (ö´-lis), a harbor town in central Greece, facing the Straits of Euboea. From there, the Greek fleet set sail for Troy after the sacrifice of Iphigenia.

24. Chalcis (kal´-kis), chief city in Euboea, located where the island comes closest to the mainland.

25. The barbarian region north of Greece, between the Danube and the Hellespont.

26. The "remedy" Artemis demanded was that Agamemnon sacrifice his daughter Iphigenia in order to obtain favorable winds to sail to Troy.

Speaking up, the elder lord
    said this: "To disregard
an oracle is grievous, but
    to kill my child is hard,
to stain my hands with maiden blood—
    to kill my home's delight.
Yet should I fail the allied fleet?
    Can either choice be right?
They want the maiden's blood to stop
    the winds. Their passions swell.
Their wild desire's natural.
    Let's hope that all goes well."

Antistrophe 4 (205–217)

But when he donned compulsion's yoke,
    his mental winds grew cold,
unholy, sacrilegious, foul.
    No action seemed too bold.
The courage of insanity's
    a fountainhead of pain.
He dared become his daughter's ex-
    ecutioner to gain
help punishing an errant wife
    and sending off his ships.

Strophe 5 (218–227)

The battle-loving lords ignore
    her pleas and maidenhood.
Not even cries of "Father!" do
    the maiden any good.
Her father prays, then gives commands.
    "Take care! Arrange her gown,
then lift her like a goat above
    the altar, facing down,
and gag her with a bridle lest
    a curse escape her lips."

Antistrophe 5 (228–237)

Her gown, a splash of saffron dye,
*   unfolds, and silent darts*
of pity that her eyes release
*   bounce off her killers' hearts.*
A lovely painting—oh but how
*   the untouched virgin longs*
to use her voice, for in the past
*   she'd lovingly sung songs:*
the third libation's paean[27] *in*
*   her father's banquet hall.*

I neither know nor say the rest,
*   though Calchas never lies*
and Justice uses suffering
*   to make some people wise.*
The future's known when it occurs.
*   Till then be full of cheer.*
It's good as weeping. Come the dawn,
*   the truth will be quite clear.*

(Turning to CLYTAEMESTRA. She has entered from
the skēnē unobtrusively during the chorus' song.)

May good ensue for Apia's[28]
*   close guard and bastion wall.*

CORYPHAEUS:
I've come to pay you homage, mighty queen.   258
It's right and just to honor royal wives

---

27. At the end of formal dinners, three libations were poured and a hymn, or paean, was sung in honor of Zeus and other gods.

28. Apia (a´-pē-ə), a name of uncertain origin for the Peloponnesus.

when husbands leave their thrones unoccupied.   260
Besides, I'd gladly learn if you have had
good news or merely offer prayers in hope
of some, though I'll respect your silence too.

CLYTAEMESTRA:
Just pray this kindly time (as people call
the night) will bear a smiling child at dawn,
and welcome happy news exceeding hopes:
the men of Greece have captured Priam's town.

CORYPHAEUS:
How's that? I'm almost deaf from disbelief!

CLYTAEMESTRA:
Troy now belongs to Hellas. Clear enough?

CORYPHAEUS:
My happiness calls forth a creeping tear.   270

CLYTAEMESTRA:
Your eye accuses you of loyalty.

CORYPHAEUS:
But is there any proof your news is true?

CLYTAEMESTRA:
Of course! Unless a god's deceiving me.

CORYPHAEUS:
Have dreams' enthralling visions swayed your mind?

CLYTAEMESTRA:
I wouldn't trust a sleeping brain's report.

CORYPHAEUS:
Then does some idle talk inflate your hopes?

CLYTAEMESTRA:
You're mocking me! Am I a little girl?

CORYPHAEUS:
How long ago was Priam's city sacked?

CLYTAEMESTRA:
Within the night that bears the coming dawn.

CORYPHAEUS:
What messenger brought word so quickly then?   280

CLYTAEMESTRA:
Hephaestus, sending beams from Ida's[29] peak.
One beacon sparked another, bringing news
like Persian couriers.[30] Mount Ida flashed
to Hermes' cliff on Lemnos.[31] Zeus's peak,
sheer Athos,[32] caught the island's giant flame.

29. A small mountain southeast of Troy. In the *Iliad*, Zeus watches the war from Ida's peak.
30. A reference to the Persians' "Royal Road," a highway 1,677 miles long running from the provincial capital of Sardis in eastern Turkey to the imperial city of Susa near the Persian Gulf. Mounted couriers operating in relays are said to have traversed the road in seven days.
31. Lemnos is a large island in the northern Aegean, west of Troy. The exact location of "Hermes' cliff" is not known.
32. Athos (a'-thōs), a mountainous promontory in northern Greece, northwest of Lemnos.

Its fire's penetrating strength then leapt
its bounds and skimmed the water's back for joy.
< . . . >[33]
A blazing pine, as though a sun, cast beams
of gold on heights of Mount Macistus[34] next.
Nor had that hill succumbed to thoughtless sleep.   290
It played the ready messenger at once.
Its light flew far across Euboea's straits,
alerting those who guard Messapium.[35]
They played their part and sent the message on,
igniting piles of withered shrubbery.
The stalwart signal, far from growing dim,
vaulted across the plain Asopus soaks,[36]
like moonbeams lunging toward Cithaeron's peaks.[37]
There it aroused another traveling flame,
for lookouts didn't spurn the distant light   300
but kindled even more than they were told.
And so it leapt the bay called Gorgon's Eye,[38]
striking the nearby goat-infested hill
and rousing it to keep the fire's law.
Sparing no effort, it creates a beard
of flame, a giant blaze that overleaps

33. One or two lines seem to be missing.

34. Macistus (mä-kis´-təs), location unknown, probably in Euboea.

35. Messapiuum (mä-sa´-pē-əm), a small mountain near the Boeotian coast, opposite Chalcis.

36. Asopus (ä-sō´-pəs), a river flowing east across Boeotia from Mount Cithaeron into the Euboean Straits south of Chalcis.

37. Cithaeron (sə-thē´-rän), a mountainous ridge, ten miles long, separating Boeotia from Athens in the southeast.

38. Reference unknown.

the cape that guards the blue Saronic strait[39]
and then descending quickly comes to rest
at Spider Hill,[40] our city's lookout place.
From there the light, grandchild of Ida's flame,   310
invades this royal house of Atreids.
Such was the relay race for beacon lights
that I devised, and they completed it,
each runner, first and last, victorious.
And that's the sort of proof I offer you,
the sign my husband sent to me from Troy.

CORYPHAEUS:
I'll thank the gods a little later on.
I'd rather listen now and gaze in awe
while you complete the story you've begun.

CLYTAEMESTRA:
Today Achaeans have control of Troy.   320
The voices there don't sing in harmony.
Fill jars with olive oil and vinegar.
They stand apart. You wouldn't call them friends.
That's how the conquered act with conquerors.
Their voices sound as different as their fates.
The former cry *Oimoi!* while some embrace

---

39. The Saronic (sə-rä´-nik) Gulf, a bay south of Attica, contains several islands, including Salamis. The reference here seems to be to some passageway between islands and shore.

40. A hill near Epidaurus, about twenty miles east of Argos. Its name is an ominous coincidence, since Clytaemestra is to be called a spider (line 1492, repeated at 1516).

dead husbands, some their brothers, some the men
who fathered them. They mourn the deaths of those
they loved. They mourn with throats no longer free.
Their battles done, the victors roam the streets   330
by night. They're hungry now and stuff themselves
with what the city has. No rationing's
involved. They get whatever luck provides,
then settle down in captive homes. They've had
enough of open air and dewy fields.
Tonight they'll sleep like happy men at peace
from dusk to dawn, no need for posting guards.
If they respect the fallen nation's gods,
their images and shrines, the chances are
that they'll avoid the captive state themselves.   340
And so let's hope the soldiers aren't inflamed
by greed to handle things they shouldn't touch.
Their safe homecoming's not assured. They've yet
to make the turn and cross the finish line.
But if they do, without offending gods,
the vengeful dead may be appeased some day—
unless new evils suddenly descend.
So much for what a woman has to say.
May Goodness win so clearly all can see.
I long to taste its many noble fruits.   350

CORYPHAEUS:
You've spoken wisely, woman, like a man
of sense. Your evidence persuaded me.
I'm ready now to praise the gods. They've paid
our labors back and done so handsomely.

>   (CLYTAEMESTRA recedes into the shadow of the palace
>   but does not exit.)

CHORUS:
King Zeus and our ally, the Night,   Anapests (355–366)
who gave us unparalleled glories,
who tossed on the towers of Troy
a netting that neither adults
nor the recently born overleapt,
slavery's impervious mesh,
the fabric of total disaster!
All honor to Zeus the hospitable,
for he was the doer. He aimed
his arrow at Paris with care,
making sure that it wouldn't fall short
or uselessly hurdle the stars overhead.

Now they can speak of Zeus's blow.   Strophe 1 (367–384)
His tracks are there for all to see.
He acted as decreed, although
a few there are who disagree.

They've said the gods no longer care
when lowly mortals boldly tread
on what is sacrosanct and fair.
That's what the impious have said.

But their descendants see the light:
some kinds of courage are a curse,
when pride attains an unjust height
and treasure vaults are like to burst.

We long for wealth without the pain.
Grant just enough for men of sense.
Against the risks of too much gain,
there's no reliable defense,

no safety for the man who kicks
the shrine of Justice down.

When wrong Persuasion, Ruin's[41] *kin,*   Antistrophe 1 (385–402)
that counselor's noxious progeny,
asserts her strength and barges in,
there's no effective remedy.

An evil act is hard to hide.
It casts an eerie, ugly light,
and when the guilty person's tried,
his brazen lies turn black as night.[42]

He's like a child who chased a bird
and caused his whole community
an evil that could not be cured.
Gods hear no prayers from such as he.

For Justice always catches those
who do what decency forbids.
That's what the case of Paris shows.
When visiting the Atreids,

he mocked all hospitality
by cuckolding his host.

---

41. The Greek word translated as "Ruin" is *Até*, a supernatural force that blinds men to the disastrous consequences of immoral actions. In the *Iliad* (19.87–92) Agamemnon blames *Até* for inducing him to take away Achilles' slave girl.

42. Inferior bronze containing an admixture of lead turns black with wear and tear.

She left alarms ("To arms! It's war!")   Strophe 2 (403–419)
throughout the city's length and breadth.
Meanwhile to Ilium she bore
a novel kind of dowry: death.

See her gaily tripping through
the city gates on tip of toe,
to dare what she'd no right to do.
The household prophets cry, "Eeoo!"

"Oh house! Oh chiefs! Oh marriage bed!
Oh loving woman's traces there!"
And yet her husband hasn't said
a word in anger, plaint, or prayer.

He yearns for one who's overseas.
A ghost now seems to rule the house.
Nor do his lovely statues please.
They're hateful to the lonely spouse.

Their lifeless eyes of marble make
a mockery of love.

Nostalgic visions come by night,   Antistrophe 2 (420–436)
They're comforting, but never stay.
When dreamers glimpse a happy sight,
it just as quickly drifts away.

Nor does it ever come again
with Sleep along his feathery way.
The sorrows that he feels within
beside his hearth are worse by day.

Elsewhere in Greece the men who dare

to journey to a foreign land
leave homes behind with doorways where
their tearful wives and mothers stand,

enduring lives of sore travail.
They love the sight of those they send
away to fight, but fear that they'll
return no longer shaped as men,

that they'll come home again transformed
to ashes stuffed in jars.

Ares, bodies' trafficker,   Strophe 3 (437–455)
holds the scale when spearmen clash
and sends their friends from Trojan pyres
heavy, hard-to-mourn-for ash.

He packs compact ceramic jars
with dust in place of flesh and bone,
while comrades weep and praise the dead,
the expertise this man had shown,

how nobly that man fought and fell,
surrendering his precious life.
Another says, beneath his breath,
"It's all because of someone's wife."

They're angry at the Atreids,
who brought the suit that caused it all.
So many handsome youths remain
in graves around the Trojan wall.

The hostile conquered land conceals
the men who conquered it.

The people's voice is angry now.   Antistrophe 3 (456–474)
Their leaders stand accurst.
The night hides something in its cloak.
I don't know what but fear the worst.

The gods keep track of those who spill
excessive blood. The time comes when
Black Furies swarm and overturn
the luck of justice-spurning men.

They grind their lives to nothingness.
There isn't anywhere to hide,
not even down among the dead.
There's danger too in vaulting pride,

for lightning strikes from Zeus's eyes.
Don't give me blessings that incur
the jealousy of other men.
I wouldn't be a conqueror,

although I'd hate to spend my life
enslaved to someone else.

CHORISTERS 1–6:
Word races through the city, spread   Epode (475–487)
by optimistic beacon flames,
but is it so? We just don't know.
Perhaps the gods are playing games.

CHORISTERS 7–12:
Who's such a child or so insane
that beacons set his heart aflame,
but when he hears a counterclaim,
he loses heart completely?

CHORISTERS 1–6:
A woman playing soldier cheers
before the battle's end appears.

CHORISTERS 7–12:
Yes, women being persuasive send
*   rumors everywhere,*
but quickly as they spread abroad
*   they vanish in the air.*

CORYPHAEUS:
We'll learn about those incandescent lamps,   489
the signal brands, and fire relays soon,   490
whether they spoke as truthful messengers
or dreams, just pleasing lights that fooled our minds.
I see a herald coming from the shore.
A wreath of olive branches shades his head.
Mud's thirsty twin, a cloud of dust, implies
he has important news. His message won't
consist of puffs of smoke from burning trees.
He'll simply speak and say, "Rejoice!" or else—
I'd rather not discuss the other choice.
I only pray that he confirms the signs   500
we've seen—and those who have a different wish
enjoy the fruit of their perverted thought.

      (Enter the HERALD.)

HERALD:
Eeoo! The Argive earth's paternal soil!

      (He falls to the ground, kisses it, then rises.)

I've come here bright and early, ten years late,

fulfilling one of many battered hopes.
I never dreamt I'd die at home and claim
a share of my beloved family tomb.
Hail earth! Hail light of sun and nation's most
exalted Zeus! Hail lord of Pytho[43] too,
no longer launching deadly darts our way.[44]   510
You raged enough beside Scamander's[45] stream,
O lord Apollo. Be a savior now
and heal our pain! Assembled gods, I call
on you and on my honor's guardian,
beloved Hermes, heralds' cynosure,[46]
and heroes, you who sent our force abroad,
now welcome our return—what's left of us.
Eeoo! It's there! The lovely hall of kings,
the council seats and gods that face the dawn!
The time is now or never! Give the king,   520
away so long, a decent greeting. Smile!
The sunshine Agamemnon brings dispels
the dark for you and all these people here.
Give him the royal welcome he deserves,
the man who leveled Troy and worked the ground
with Zeus's pick, the justice-bringing god.
Gone are their altars; gone their temples too.
The very seeds of life have been destroyed.
And he who strapped this yoke on Trojan necks,

---

43. "Pytho" is another name for Delphi, the site of the oracle of Apollo.

44. A reference to the beginning of the *Iliad* (1.43–52): Apollo attacks the Greek camp with arrows that bring a plague because Agamemnon has refused to accept a ransom in return for releasing the daughter of a priest of Apollo.

45. A river rising in Mount Ida and passing Troy en route to the sea.

46. The *Homeric Hymn to Hermes* describes the young god's acquisition of the role of herald.

the blessed elder son of Atreus, 530
the paragon of modern men, comes home!
Paris and his complicit city boast
no more of acts surpassing sufferings.
That proven thief and rapist has his just
reward. His booty's gone. All thanks to him,
his father's house lies level with the ground.
The Priamids[47] paid double for his crimes.

CORYPHAEUS:
Achaean army's messenger, be well!

HERALD:
I am. Now I can die a happy man.

CORYPHAEUS:
Was longing for this country hard to bear? 540

HERALD:
So hard my eyes are dripping tears of joy.

CORYPHAEUS:
We'd say you caught a pleasing illness then.

HERALD:
How so? I need your help to master that.

CORYPHAEUS:
The love you suffered from was mutual.

47. The children of Priam, king of Troy: Paris, his heroic brother
Hector, the prophetess Cassandra, and many others, since Priam had children
by several wives.

HERALD:
The army longed for those who longed for them?

CORYPHAEUS:
We often groaned aloud with broken hearts.

HERALD:
What caused the people bitterness like that?

CORYPHAEUS:
Of old I've found that silence helps my health.

HERALD:
With rulers gone, did others stir your fear?

CORYPHAEUS:
So much that now, like you, we'd welcome death.   550

HERALD:
Because things ended well? It took some time.
In certain ways, you'd call us fortunate.
In others, cursed; but who—excepting gods
—enjoys a life entirely free of pain?
If I described the hardships we endured,
the narrow benches where we tried to sleep—
what misery was not our daily lot?
And once we landed, things got even worse.
Our beds were by the hostile walls of Troy,
a meadow where the unrelenting drops   560
of dew from earth and sky were constant grief
and filled our woolen clothes with hungry bugs.
The birds all died when winter rolled around,
and Ida's snow made camp unbearable.

In summer's heat the sea would fall asleep,
as though it napped, and lie there deathly still.
But why rehearse these things? Our labor's done.
It's truly done. At least, the men who died
will never have to leave their bunks again.   569
As for the Argive soldiers who survive,[48]   573
our profits win: they're not outweighed by grief.   574
So why consider those who died at all?   570
Should Fortune's malice trouble living men?   571
I bid a long farewell to tragic tears.   572
It fits this sunny day for us whose fame   575
takes flight to publish boasts[49] instead—to wit:
"Achaea's army, having conquered Troy
in days gone by, attached these gleaming spoils
of war to temple walls throughout the land."
One thing is certain: those who read such words   580
will give the generals and city praise
and honor Zeus's kindness. That is all.

CORYPHAEUS:
I don't deny that you've persuaded me.
An open mind retains its youthful glow
even when old. The royal house and queen
gain most from this, but I'll be wealthy too.

(CLYTAEMESTRA comes forward to speak.)

48. The scribe seems to have skipped lines 570 and 571 initially and then
inserted them three lines later, making them 573 and 574, respectively. The
correct order was restored in D. L. Page's *Aeschyli, Septem quae supersunt
tragoedias.*

49. Victorious soldiers donated some of their booty (e.g., enemy armor)
to temples, with inscriptions commemorating their accomplishments.

CLYTAEMESTRA:
I raised a joyous cry some time ago,
once I had seen my blazing messenger
announcing Ilium's defeat last night.
Some people scoffed. "Have beacon-watching slaves   590
persuaded you that Troy has fallen now?
A woman's hopes are easily aroused!"
Their implication was: I'd lost my mind.
But I kept on, and women's ways prevailed.
Throughout the city happy shouts rang out,
praising the gods. In temples, incense lulled
the aromatic, sacrificial flames.
What need have I of further words from you?
I'll get the story straight from royal lips.
Right now I long to give my reverend spouse   600
the grandest welcome home when he arrives.
What brighter day does any woman see
than when she opens gates to greet her man
returning safe from war? So tell him that,
while urging haste. The city loves him so.
Let him return to find a faithful wife,
the same he left behind, the household dog,
her master's friend, but fierce to enemies,
and loyal every other way. In all
this time, I didn't break a single seal.   610
I don't know any more of other men
or scandals than I do of dipping bronze.
So much for truthful boasting. Nothing's wrong
with such displays when noble women speak.

CORYPHAEUS:
So says the queen. Correctly understood,
that speech was one of seemly sentiments.

But tell us more, good herald. What about
how Menelaus fares? Did *he* come back,
our nation's fortress, safe and sound with you?

HERALD:
I have no happy tale to tell his friends,   620
not one that they'd enjoy for very long.

CORYPHAEUS:
It's good when true and happy coincide.
Their disagreement's rather hard to hide.

HERALD:
The man and vessel both have disappeared,
gone from the army. There you have the true.

CORYPHAEUS:
Did he set forth alone from Trojan shores,
or did a giant storm make off with him?

HERALD:
Bull's-eye! The latter. You've impaled a great
misfortune using no unneeded words.

CORYPHAEUS:
What did the other sailors have to say?   630
Did they pronounce him dead or living still?

HERALD:
Nobody knows a thing—unless you count
lord Helios,[50] who nourishes the earth.

50. The sun personified.

CORYPHAEUS:
You say a storm—the work of heaven's wrath,
no doubt—attacked the fleet, then settled down?

HERALD:
One shouldn't stain a happy day with tales
like this. It's not the way to honor gods.
Suppose a gloomy messenger arrived
reporting sad events. "The army flees!"
"The state has suffered one collective wound,   640
and many homes have sacrificed their man,
for that's the double lash that Ares loves,
twin spears of ruin, bloody steeds of death."
The hellish hymn I have to sing would suit
a man already packing grief like that.
But what about a smiling messenger
informing cheerful folks of victories?
Must I pollute my happy news with ill?
Report a storm that heaven's anger shaped?
Well—sea and fire, bitter foes before,   650
resolving differences revealed their pact
by ruining the Argives' luckless fleet.
The evil, swelling sea awoke by night.
Then ships colliding broke in Thracian winds,
were buffeted by cyclones, drenched by rain.
Our friends were gone entirely, out of sight,
lost to the maelstrom's wicked shepherding.
When Helios's light returned, we saw
Aegean waters bloom with tattered sails
and broken spars—and dead Achaean men.   660
And yet some trick or supplication saved
our ship and us. Some god, no human, took
the helm and brought us safely through the storm.
Good Fortune occupied our rowing bench.
We weren't immersed in surging waves when moored;

we never ran aground on stony reefs.
In short, we gave the deadly sea the slip.
Next day we hardly credited our luck,
and recent suffering still haunted us.
The pounding seas had overwhelmed our fleet.   670
Yet if those other crews are still alive,
they surely think that *we* were lost at sea,
the very thing that we assume of them.
Hope for the best. Especially hope for this:
that Menelaus somehow reached the shore.
If he still bathes in sunshine anywhere,
alive and conscious thanks to Zeus's art,
who may not wish to wipe his family out,
there is some hope that he'll be coming home.
That isn't much to claim, but it's the truth.   680

(Exit HERALD, CLYTAEMESTRA recedes.)

CHORUS:
Who's the one who gave her such   Strophe 1 (681–698)
    an all-too-fitting name?
One unseen, perhaps, who chose
    his words with perfect aim,

knowing well ahead of time
    the things that had to be,
naming Helen "Helen" as
    a kind of prophecy:

battle bride and source of strife
    and truly hell[51] *on ships.*

---

51. In Greek, the first syllable of Helen's name, *hel-*, is also a verbal root meaning "seize" or "destroy." The chorus calls her *helenaus* (ship-destroyer), *helandros* (man-destroyer), and *heleptolis* (city-destroyer).

Hell on men and city too,
    when blasts from Zephyr's[52] *lips*

parted fine-spun draperies,
    and she herself set sail.
Many armored hunters tracked
    her rowers' vanished trail,

after she and Paris reached
    the leafy Simoïs.[53]
All of that because of Strife,
    whom bloody conflicts please.

Heaven's potent anger forged   Antistrophe 1 (699–716)
    a bond indeed that day,
bound the town of Ilium
    in later times to pay

for sins against the persons who
    provided bed and board,
Zeus's laws of guest and host
    disgracefully ignored!

Those who sang the bridal hymn,
    pronouncing it with pride,
paid a price for having been
    the in-laws of the bride.

Priam's ancient city learned
    to sing a mournful song,

---

52. Zephyr (ze´-fər), the west wind personified.
53. Simois (si´-mō-ēz), a stream near Troy, one of Scamander's tributaries.

calling Paris one who lay
*   where he did not belong.*

He began an age of tears.
*   He brought the city low.*
Thanks to him the citizens'
*   unhappy blood would flow.*

Just so a man once brought a lion home,   Strophe 2 (717–726)
a suckling cub, to raise it as his own.
still fond of nursing, easily controlled,
immature, a joy for young and old.
The man would hold this creature of the wild
in loving arms as though a newborn child.
Its stomach made the usual demands.
It fawned bright-eyed and ate from human hands.

In time a change to inborn traits took place,   Antistrophe 2 (727–735)
and it repaid its foster parents' grace
by raining death on flocks of goats and sheep,
an uninvited diner. Blood ran deep.
The house was soaked, and nothing could deter
the fatal bane, the all-out massacre.
A god-sent priest of ruin had been nursed
inside that house, and all therein were cursed.

One might call what came to Troy   Strophe 3 (736–749)
*   a dream of cloudless skies,*
riches' soothing ornament,
*   the darts of bashful eyes,*
Love's heart-breaking bloom, but she
*   would swerve, and they would learn*
how a happy wedding feast
*   could take a bitter turn.*

Moving into Priam's home,
     she proved to be a most
troublesome inhabitant.
     The god of guest and host
sent her as a Fury there
     to break the hearts of brides.

There's a hoary proverb that
     descends from days gone by:
splendid human fortunes grown
     to greatness never die
lacking progeny. In fact,
     good fortune always sows
quenchless grief for families,
     a garden full of woes.
My opinion isn't that.
     I have a different view
Evil acts are what beget
     those later evils too.
Houses governed justly have
     good fortune, so say I.

Among the evils people do,
ancient outrage[54] *leads to new.*
It happens late or straightaway.
On the designated day,
a demon comes that one can't fight,
reckless Ruin black as night,
and dark descends. A person sees
family similarities.

---

54. The Greek word is *hubris*, which is used both of ethically outrageous actions and of the spiritual disposition, arrogance perhaps, that lies behind them.

Justice lights the smoky den. Antistrophe 4 (772–781)
She honors poor but righteous men,
passing gilded mansions by
with quickened step, averted eye;
for they were built by dirty hands.
It's cleanliness that she demands.
Gleaming riches just offend.
With her, things reach their proper end.

    (Enter AGAMEMNON in a chariot, accompanied by
CASSANDRA.)

Hail Atreid monarch, the man Anapests (782–809)
who leveled the city of Troy!
What reverent term should I use
to name you that doesn't exceed
the courtesy owed to a king
and doesn't fall short of the mark?
To the many whose ways are unjust
appearance is better than truth.
You suffer misfortune; they all
take part in the weeping, and yet
they don't feel the sting in their hearts.
They also rejoice when you're glad,
distorting their faces with smiles,
but looks can't deceive an adept
appraiser of flocks, even though
they mimic the kindest intentions
and wheedle with watery love.
When you were collecting the troops
on Helen's account—to be frank—
my picture of you wasn't kind.
Your feelings seemed out of control.
You'd sacrifice masculine lives

to win a promiscuous wife!
But now from the depth of my heart
with genuine love I can say,
Hurrah for the men who completed the task!

In time, by conducting inquiries, you'll learn
which citizens staying in the city were just
and which of them weren't.

AGAMEMNON:
It's right to greet the land of Argos first   810
and my accomplices, its native gods,
my escorts home, who helped me get my just
revenge on Priam's town. We pled our case
by killing, not by talk, nor were the gods
divided. Pebbles filled the bloody urn
marked "Troy's complete destruction."[55] Hope alone,
no heavy hand, approached the other jar.
Smoke marks the spot the fallen city stood.
The storm of Ruin lives. One whiffs their wealth
in puffs of dust that burst from smoldering ash.   820
We owe the gods long-lasting gratitude.
We've gotten our revenge for brazen rape.
A woman caused it all. Because of her
the Argive jaws, the Horse's progeny,
the armored legions, crushed a city-state.
The Pleiades were setting[56] when we struck.
A hungry lion leapt the battlements

55. Agamemnon speaks as though the gods voted on Troy's fate in the
manner of Athenian voters: by dropping pebbles into an appropriate urn.

56. I.e., it was very late at night, toward dawn. The Pleiades (plē´-ə-dēz),
also known as the Seven Sisters, are a cluster of seven stars identified with the
daughters of Atlas.

of Troy and drank its fill of royal blood.
So there's my lengthy prelude thanking gods.
I noted what you said and quite agree.   830
I'd testify that your opinion's true.
Few have the gift of praising friends' success
without conceiving pangs of jealousy.
For one who suffers some disease, the heart's
malicious poison doubles grief and pain.
As though his own afflictions weren't enough,
he's tortured by the sight of others' health.
I know whereof I speak. My closest friends
so-called were mostly shallow counterfeits,
mere shadows, fleeting images of friends.   840
Except one man who didn't wish to sail:
Odysseus. He became my favorite horse,
and now he's either dead—or maybe not.
About the gods and city government,
we'll gather all the citizens and learn
what's working well and how to guarantee
that beneficial dispositions last;
and where there's need for healing remedies,
we'll cauterize or cut with special care
to extirpate whatever causes pain.   850
But first, being home, my rafters overhead,
my hearth nearby, I'd better greet the gods
who sent me forth and finally brought me back.
Success attended me. I hope it stays.

(CLYTAEMESTRA comes forward.)

CLYTAEMESTRA:
Men! Citizens, you Argive elders here,
I will not shrink from telling you about
my husband-loving ways. In time one's fear

of public speaking fades, and what I'll say
is hardly second-hand, for I'll describe
my wretched life while he campaigned at Troy.   860
A woman suffers dreadfully at home,
alone, without her husband, constantly
alarmed by new, malicious rumors, each
portending greater grief. They never stop.
The household never has a quiet day.
If he'd received as many wounds as word
thereof came streaming home, he'd be more like
a fishing net, with nothing left but holes.
To die as often as they said he did,
would take a triple-bodied Geryon,[57]   870
and he could boast of having donned a cloak
of dirt three times, each body buried once,
with ample soil above and more below.
Why, thanks to those incessant false reports,
I often strapped a noose around my neck,
and others had to free me forcibly.

(To AGAMEMNON.)

And that's the reason that the boy's not here,
who guarantees our common trust and love.
I mean, of course, Orestes. Never fear.
In fact, a friend and ally's raising him,   880
the Phocian Strophius.[58] He spoke at length
about our dangers, yours at Troy and here,
the danger that the noisy mob might weave

57. Geryon (jər´-i-ən), a three-bodied giant slain by Heracles.

58. Phocis is a territory in central Greece adjoining Mount Parnassus.
Strophius is said in later sources to have been married to a sister of
Agamemnon. Strophius' son, Pylades, became Orestes' best friend and
companion.

an evil plot. It's only human, so
he said, to kick a man who's lying down.
That's my excuse. There's nothing hidden there.
My eyes were gushing fountains once, but now
they're dry, completely. Not a drop remains.
What's more, I'm nearly blind from keeping watch
at night for news of you and shedding tears   890
at idle beacon lights. The gentle hum
of insect wings would trumpet me from dreams,
in which I saw you wounded many times
for every moment spent in restless sleep.
All that is over now.

     (To the CORYPHAEUS.)

                 With carefree heart,
I call this man our barnyard dog, the rope
that holds our mast, the pillar underneath
our lofty roof, a father's only son,
a shore that's glimpsed by desperate mariners,   900
a brilliant sunrise following a storm,
a fountain that a thirsty traveler finds.
(Escaping all constraints is oh so sweet!)[59]
He surely merits titles such as those.
But Envy, stay away! We've undergone
much suffering.

     (To AGAMEMNON.)

           And now, sweet husband, leave
your chariot—without permitting feet
that trampled Troy to touch the lowly earth.

59. This line is probably an interpolation that originated as a marginal
citation of a parallel to Clytaemestra's sentiments.

(ATTENDANTS enter from the palace carrying purple
tapestries.)

Why are you waiting, girls? You've gotten your
instructions. Spread his path with tapestries.
Be quick! Provide a purple passageway.   910

(The ATTENDANTS obey.)

Let Justice lead him home against all odds.
As for the rest, my sleepless care will see
that what the gods ordain is justly done.

AGAMEMNON:
Daughter of Leda,[60] household's guardian,
your speech was like my absence: very long.
Long and improper. Words of praise like those
are gifts that ought to come from other men.
As for the rest, don't use a woman's ways
to soften me. We're not barbarians.
Spare me your servile shouts and groveling!   920
Don't pave my path with clothing. It'll cause
resentment. Honors such as that belong to gods.
For one who's mortal that's a dangerous thing
to do—to trample fine embroideries.
Just honor me as human, not divine.
Our language makes the differences between
fine woven works and foot towels clear. No gift
from god beats lucid thought! That man
alone is blest whose life has ended well.
My courage comes from honoring such truths.   930

60. Clytaemestra and Helen were daughters of Leda (lē′-də), queen of
Sparta, who was visited by Zeus in the form of a swan.

CLYTAEMESTRA:
I have one question. Speaking candidly . . .

AGAMEMNON:
I won't conceal my feelings, rest assured.

CLYTAEMESTRA (indicating the tapestries):
Would you have offered these to gods from fear?

AGAMEMNON:
If some religious expert told me to.

CLYTAEMESTRA:
If Priam conquered, what would he have done?

AGAMEMNON:
He would have trampled all of them with glee!

CLYTAEMESTRA:
Then you should not be cowed by people's talk!

AGAMEMNON:
And yet the people's voice is powerful.

CLYTAEMESTRA:
If you're not envied, you're not admirable!

AGAMEMNON:
This lust for combat isn't womanly!   940

CLYTAEMESTRA:
Even defeat becomes successful men.

AGAMEMNON:
Are you intent on winning this debate?

CLYTAEMESTRA:
Be master still and freely choose to lose.

AGAMEMNON:
If that's your pleasure. Someone! Quick! Undo
my shoes, the servile mats beneath my feet.

(CLYTAEMESTRA'S ATTENDANTS obey.)

May no god's jealous eye catch sight of me
crushing these robes of seaborne purple dye.
We purchased them with silver. What a shame
to ruin household wealth with one's own feet!
So much for that. Please take this foreign girl   950
inside, but gently. God[61] is well-disposed
toward those who treat their subjects graciously.
Nobody volunteers for slavery's yoke.
What's more, the girl is mine, the army's gift,
a blossom mid our many spoils of war.
And now, since you've defeated me, observe:
I march inside on purple luxuries.

(Exit AGAMEMNON into the palace.)

CLYTAEMESTRA (addressing AGAMEMNON as he leaves):
The sea is there, and who will empty it?
It breeds abundant purple ooze as good

61. The Greeks often referred to "god" without an article, which makes
them sound to us like monotheists. It seems, however, that they used "god"
as a collective term for the gods in general, just as we use "man" to refer to
mankind or the human race.

as silver, dye that's endlessly renewed.[62]   960
We have the means to fix the damage, lord.
This household can't conceive of being poor,
and I'd have vowed to trample many robes,
if oracles demanded such an act,
when I was seeking ways to save your life.
When roots survive, the leafy branch returns,
providing shade from Sirius[63] the dog.
By coming back to your domestic hearth,
you promise warmth in wintertime. Likewise,
when Zeus is making wine from bitter grapes,   970
a breath of cooling air will fill the house
because the master's lingering therein.
Lord of fulfillment, Zeus, fulfill my prayers.
Take care to finish that which you've begun.

> (Exit CLYTAEMESTRA with ATTENDANTS into the
> palace.)

CHORUS:

Why does this constant fear fly round   Strophe 1 (975–987)
    my omen-wary heart?
Why do I hear unpaid, unbidden
    songs of mantic art?
Why can't my courage spit them out
    like some confusing dream,
and be convincing? Why does it

62. Purple dye was a highly prized luxury item manufactured from the
secretions of sea snails now known as murices.

63. The appearance of Sirius (sir´-ē-əs), the Dog Star, in mid-August
marked the beginning of the hottest season of the year.

no longer reign supreme?
Some time has passed since mooring ropes
    disturbed the quiet sand,
and seaborne warriors from Greece
    set sail for Trojan land.

I saw him coming back myself.   Antistrophe 1 (988–1000)
    I witnessed that event,
and yet my unschooled spirit sings
    a lyreless lament,
a Fury's song. The cheer that hope
    begets has gone away.
I fear my inner voices have
    important things to say.
My reeling heart and conscience feel
    some crisis must be near;
and yet I pray my fears are false
    and simply disappear.

The goal of perfect health   Strophe 2 (1001–1016)
recedes forevermore.
Disease comes bursting in.
It owns the house next door.
Though life is right on course,
[one's not immune to grief.
How often sturdy ships][64]
have struck a hidden reef.
If caution casts away
some precious little thing,

64. Several words are missing in the manuscript. The bracketed words are my conjectural restoration of the thought.

some jewel,[65] ahead of time
with moderation's sling,
the household won't collapse
from sheer satiety.
The ship won't settle on
the bottom of the sea.
And Zeus is generous;
his kindness never fails.
From furrows every year
he cures what hunger ails.

But once a victim's blood   Antistrophe 2 (1017 1034)
has turned the ground to black
beneath a killer's feet,
whose spell will call it back?
The only one who knew
a death-reversing charm
was quieted by Zeus
on terms not free of harm.[66]
If laws of Fate ordained
by heaven were not such
that Fate prevents a man
from gaining far too much,

65. Apparently a reference to the story of Polycrates, a wealthy tyrant, who threw his favorite ring into the sea to ward off divine jealousy. Unfortunately, the ring was returned to him inside a fish, and he ended up being tortured to death by a rival. The classical version of the tale is found in Herodotus 3.39–43, 120–125.

66. Apollo's son Asclepius, a great healer, was slain by Zeus's lightning when he attempted to bring a dead man back to life; see Pindar, *Pythian* 3.47–60.

my heart would guide my tongue
and bring the truth to light;
but now its only course
is muttering by night.[67]
My heart is aching. There's
no hope that I can find
the needed words, although
a fire heats my mind.

(Enter CLYTAEMESTRA from the palace.)

CLYTAEMESTRA:
Come in, Cassandra. I'm addressing you.   1035
By Zeus's gracious ordinance, you'll join
our household's lustral rites at altar's side
and take your place among our many slaves.
Step down from there. Forget your royal airs.
Even Alcmene's child was sold, they say,   1040
and ate the barley loaves of servitude.[68]
When such misfortune falls to someone's lot,
a master's ancient wealth is comforting.
For people gaining unexpected wealth
are always cruel to slaves. [A house as rich   1045a

---

67. The chorus seems to mean that Agamemnon is doomed by the laws of Fate that exclude excessive good fortune, especially when it is acquired by spilling blood. If he were not already doomed, they would warn him of the dangers surrounding him.

68. Alcmene's child was Heracles. Zeus punished him with slavery for an outburst of temper in which he treacherously killed a youth and for subsequently going berserk in Apollo's temple at Delphi. Heracles' owner for a year or more was Omphale, queen of Lydia. In the fully evolved version of the story, they become lovers and trade gender roles.

as ours treats servants well,] obeying the rules.[69]   1045b
From us you'll get what custom says you should.   1046

  (Prolonged silence.)

CORYPHAEUS (addressing CASSANDRA):
Her speech has ended, clearly meant for you.
Caught in a deadly trap, you should obey,
if you're persuaded. Yet, perhaps, you're not.

CLYTAEMESTRA:
Unless she chirps the way that swallows do,   1050
speaking an unknown foreign tongue, my words
have reached her mind, and they're convincing her.

CORYPHAEUS (addressing CASSANDRA):
Under the circumstances, what she says
is best. Obey and leave your carriage now.

CLYTAEMESTRA:
I haven't any time to waste out here.
The sacrificial lambs already stand
before the inner hearth, where we've prepared
the rite of thanks we thought we'd never see.

  (To CASSANDRA.)

If you'd participate, don't linger there!
Or if you're ignorant of human speech   1060
then gesture! Wave your foreign hand instead!

---

69. One or more lines are missing from the manuscript. Words in brackets are my conjectural restoration. They create a new line of text.

CORYPHAEUS:
The stranger needs a good interpreter,
it seems. She's like a captive animal.

CLYTAEMESTRA:
I'd say she's mad and hearing evil things.
She's left her newly conquered town behind
and cannot bear a bridle yet. She won't
until her mouth is wet with bloody foam.
But I won't take her insults anymore.

(Exit CLYTAEMESTRA into the palace.)

CORYPHAEUS (to CASSANDRA):
I speak in pity, not in anger. Come,
poor girl. You have to leave your carriage now.   1070
Accept this new but necessary yoke.

(CASSANDRA leaves her chariot.)

CASSANDRA:
Otótototoí popoí dá!   Strophe 1 (1072–1073)
Apollo! Apollo!

CORYPHAEUS:
Your wailing has to do with Loxias?[70]   1074
How so? He isn't one for mournful songs.   1075

CASSANDRA:
Otótototoí popoí dá!   Antistrophe 1 (1076–1077)
Apollo! Apollo!

---

70. Loxias is an alternative name for Apollo, possibly related to the adjective *loxos*, meaning slanting or oblique, a reference to his cryptic oracular pronouncements.

CORYPHAEUS:
Another inappropriate appeal!   1078
Apollo's not supposed to hear laments.   1079

CASSANDRA:
Apollo! Apollo!   Strophe 2 (1080–1082)
Lord of the streets! Apollo means destroyer![71]
This makes the second time that you're undoing me!

CORYPHAEUS:
Her own unhappy fate's her topic now.   1083
She's chattel, but a god's inside her mind.   1084

CASSANDRA:
Apollo! Apollo!   Antistrophe 2 (1085–1087)
Lord of the streets! Apollo means destroyer!
Where have you led me now? What palace do I see?

CORYPHAEUS:
I'll tell you if you're really unaware.   1088
The Atreids'! You'll find I haven't lied.   1089

CASSANDRA:
Say godless slaughterhouse instead,   Strophe 3 (1090–1092)
say witness to unending horror,
where kinsmen strike each other dead
and drops of blood adorn the floor.

CORYPHAEUS:
This foreign woman's sense of smell is like   1093
a hound's, and she'll detect some murders soon.   1094

71. An untranslatable pun in the Greek. Cassandra refers to Apollo as her *apollōn*, which can be interpreted as the proper name "Apollo" in the nominative case but also looks like a present participle of the verb meaning "destroy."

CASSANDRA:

I'm confident. I base my words   Antistrophe 3 (1095–1097)
on what I see, the wretched state
of little children massacred,
the roasted flesh their father ate.[72]

CORYPHAEUS:

Oh yes, we've heard of your prophetic fame,   1098
but there's no opening for prophets here.   1099

CASSANDRA:

Eeoo popoi! What plot's afoot?   Strophe 4 (1100–1104)
   What new distress is here?
Great ill, unbearable for those
   to whom the house is dear,
an injury that can't be healed,
   and no defender near.

CORYPHAEUS:

Now I'm perplexed by that. Her other words   1105
told tales the city speaks of openly.   1106

CASSANDRA:

Io, you wretch! Have you the strength   Antistrophe 4 (1107–1111)
   to carry out the deed?
Once you've bathed your loving spouse
   . . . but how can I proceed?
It's coming soon. One hand of yours
   will follow; one will lead.

---

72. During their feud, Atreus killed the children of his brother Thyestes and tricked him into eating their flesh.

CORYPHAEUS:
I still can't grasp her meaning. Prophecies 1112
obscured by riddles only puzzle me. 1113

CASSANDRA:
Papai! Papai! What's this I see? Strophe 5 (1114–1124)
  What deadly trap is there?
The loving wife's a hunting net,
  a homicidal snare.
The thirsty god of family strife
  should cheer because the price
is death by public stoning for
  this kind of sacrifice.

CORYPHAEUS:
What sort of Fury ought to cheer at that? 1119
You haven't put my mind at ease at all. 1120

CHORUS:
My heart! The yellow bile's come near,[73]
like someone stricken by a spear
who knows his light will disappear.
The end comes quickly then.

CASSANDRA:
Oh keep the cow and bull apart, Antistrophe 5 (1125–1135)
  lest otherwise, be warned!
She traps the bull in woven robes.

73. In ancient Greek medicine, yellow bile was one of the body's four humors. It was principally associated with anger, but, as this passage shows, it was thought that an excess of yellow bile in the vicinity of the heart caused loss of consciousness; see Hippocrates, *On Diseases* 2.5.

She takes her hidden horn.
She strikes. He falls where waters wash
　　his wounded body clean,
a basin built for taking baths,
　　a clever death machine.

CORYPHAEUS:

I never could interpret oracles,　　　　　　　　　1130
but that sounds rather ominous to me.　　　　　　　1131

CHORUS:

What good has ever come of these
verbose, ill-sounding prophecies?
They only rob our hearts of ease
by teaching us new fear.

CASSANDRA:

Io! Io! What evil fates appear!　　　　　Strophe 6 (1136–1145)
For I lament my own misfortune too.
Why did you lead this wretched woman here?
To die with him? What else is there to do?

CHORUS:

You've lost your mind or you're possessed.
You mourn yourself in tuneless song,
as nightingales who never rest
sing "Itys! Itys!" all night long.
He had the saddest sort of death,
for both his parents did him wrong.[74]

74. A reference to the myth of the sisters Procne and Philomela. The former was married to the Thracian king Tereus. He raped Philomela and

CASSANDRA:
How fortunate the nightingale appears!   Antistrophe 6 (1146–1155)
The gods have made her light and feathery
and granted sweet existence free of tears.
A cleaver's sharp division waits for me.

CHORUS:
What god approaches, causing these
outbursts of futile grief and pain?
They're fearful things, your melodies,
your shrill and ominous refrain,
the evil that your soul foresees.
Who guides you through this rough terrain?

CASSANDRA:
Io! the wedding Paris had,   Strophe 7 (1156–1166)
*   by which his friends were cursed!*
Io! Scamander's stream, at which
*   my father quenched his thirst,*
and it was on your banks that this
*   ill-fated girl was nursed.*

I think I'll soon be chanting oracles   1160
by Acheron or where Cocytus flows.[75]   1161

---

cut off her tongue when she came to visit her sister. In revenge, the sisters murdered Tereus' son by Procne, Itys, and fed his flesh to his father. The gods then transformed the threesome into birds, whose song "Itys! Itys!" is really a lament for the slain child.

75. Acheron (a´-kə-rön) and Cocytus (kō-sī´-təs) are rivers in the underworld.

CHORUS:
Your speech is far too lucid now.
A little child would comprehend.
My heart is stung at hearing how
you weep foreseeing a painful end.
It's shattering to listen to.

CASSANDRA:
Io! my fallen city! What   Antistrophe 7 (1167–1177)
     ordeals you did abide!
Io! what sacrificial beasts
     my father burned outside
the city walls. No cure was found
     in anything he tried.

He couldn't change the town's unhappy fate,   1171
and soon my flowing blood will warm the ground.   1172

CHORUS:
That comes of what you've said before.
Some heavy-handed godlike thing,
ill-willed, compels you evermore
to sing of fatal suffering.
I'm at a loss to know the end.

CASSANDRA:
No longer shall my divination peek   1178
through veils as though a newly wedded bride.
You'll feel me like a brilliant wind that blows   1180
at sunrise, drives great breakers toward the shore,
and leaves more sorrow there than came before.
I won't instruct in riddles anymore.
Now watch me as I run my quarry down.
I'm hot upon the scent of ancient crime.

A choir never leaves this house. It sings
displeasing melodies with evil words,
a band of kindred Furies always there,
carousing, bold from having drunk the blood
of human beings. They won't be sent away.   1190
The song they're singing fills the royal house.
They sing how madness started, spewing hate
of one who breached his brother's marriage bed.[76]
Is that on target? How's my archery?
Am I a pseudo-prophet, banging doors
and spouting nonsense? Swear you haven't heard
the tales of ancient crime inside this house!

CORYPHAEUS:
And how would such an oath, however firm,
heal any wounds? But I admire you.
You talk about this foreign town like one   1200
who's always dwelt nearby, not raised abroad.

CASSANDRA:
Apollo, seer god, empowered me.

CORYPHAEUS:
May we assume desire laid him low?

CASSANDRA:
There was a time this topic made me blush.

CORYPHAEUS:
Prosperity gives everybody airs.

---

76. Thyestes seduced Atreus' wife in the early stages of the brothers'
feud.

CASSANDRA:
Let's say we had a pleasant wrestling match.

CORYPHAEUS:
An act of procreation at the end?

CASSANDRA:
I promised that but cheated Loxias.

CORYPHAEUS:
Did you possess inspired skills by then?

CASSANDRA:
I told my people all their future grief.   1210

CORYPHAEUS:
And Loxias's anger did no harm?

CASSANDRA:
My words lacked all persuasion once I sinned.

CORYPHAEUS:
But what you say convinces us at least.

CASSANDRA:
Eeoo! Eeoo! O! O! What evil's here!
Once more the pain of mantic knowledge drives
my mind in circles. Dire preludes sound.
Ah! See those youngsters crouching near the house?
Those figures somewhat dim as seen in dreams?
Dead children slain, you'd think, by enemies,
and this is clear: their hands are weighted down   1220
with flesh, a family meal, intestines, hearts,
and lungs. Some passed their father's lips. How sad!
A person planning punishment for this,

a feeble beast, a stay-at-home, awaits
the lord's arrival, snuggling in bed.
("*My* lord's." I bear the yoke of slavery now.)
The admiral who leveled Troy will meet   1227
his evil fate, his stealthy ruin, soon.[77]   1230
He doesn't understand what lies behind   1228
the hateful smiling bitch's self-defense.   1229
So bold! A female murdering a male!   1231
She is—a what? What title's accurate?
A beast? A snake with heads on either end,
a Scylla[78] lying on rocks, the sailors' bane,
a raging mother sent from hell to wage
unceasing war against her own? And how
she cheered like someone routing enemies,
while feigning happiness at his return.
Who cares if I'm persuading you or not?
The future's on its way, and then you'll call   1240
my prophecies too true and pity me.

CORYPHAEUS:
Knowing about Thyestes that he dined
on children's flesh, I shook with fear to hear
that story truly told in simple terms.
I'm having trouble following the rest.

CASSANDRA:
I say you'll witness Agamemnon's death.

77. In the manuscripts the sentence spanning lines 1227 to 1230 seems obviously corrupt. A solution suggested by David Raeburn and Oliver Thomas in their *The "Agamemnon" of Aeschylus: A Commentary for Students* is to transpose line 1230 between lines 1227 and 1228. That leaves the sentence grammatically incomplete, but the general thought is easy to supply.

78. Scylla (si´-lə), a many-headed monster who devoured six of Odysseus' men.

CORYPHAEUS:
Poor woman! Be propitious! Calm your tongue!

CASSANDRA:
It's not a healing god that guides my speech.

CORYPHAEUS:
Not if your statement's true. We pray it's not.

CASSANDRA:
You pray, but they're devoted murderers.   1250

CORYPHAEUS:
Who is the man who'll do the dreadful deed?

CASSANDRA:
How short you fall of understanding me!

CORYPHAEUS:
I'd like to know what method he'll employ.

CASSANDRA:
I pride myself on speaking Greek quite well.

CORYPHAEUS:
Like Delphi: Greek but hard to understand.

CASSANDRA:
Papai! The heat! The fire's coming now!
Otoi! Wolf-god Apollo! Grief and woe!
The human lioness, who takes a wolf
to bed because her noble lion's gone,
will be my killer, be the sorceress   1260
who brims my cup with deadly poison too,

who whets her homicidal sword and boasts
that blood will pay for his possessing me.
This costume makes me laugh! These clothes,
this staff, these woolen ribbons round my neck!
At least I'll ruin them before I die!

>   (CASSANDRA removes an outer robe and tears ribbons
>   off her neck.)

Lie there in dirt! Accept my payment. *This!*

>   (She grinds her robe into the ground with her feet.)

Go make some other woman rich in grief.

>   (A gust of wind blows her discarded robe away.)[79]

Well, look at that! Apollo's stripping me
of mantic garb himself. He merely watched   1270
while I was roundly scorned and ridiculed
in all that luxury by hostile friends
[for simply prophesying truthful things.][80]
What followed was a life of poverty
and homelessness, a starving vagabond's.
And now the Prophet takes his prophet's life.

79. There are few stage directions in the inherited Greek text. The ones
printed in translations are the translator's conjectures. This passage seems to
require some physical action. Cassandra has removed articles of clothing herself, stomped on them, and told them to make some other woman miserable.
Then at lines 1269–1270, she says, in a prosaic translation, "Behold, Apollo
himself (is) the one stripping me of prophetic clothing."

80. A line seems to have fallen out of the text here. The words in brackets
are my conjectural reconstruction.

He's making me confront my deadly fate.
That "family altar's" just a chopping block.
My sacrificial blood will heat the stone.
Yet we'll not die dishonored by the gods.
Another instrument of vengeance comes,   1280
a matricide, a father's vengeful sprout.
At first a roaming exile, he'll return
to cap his family's history of crime.
The gods have sworn a solemn oath—to wit:
his father's supine corpse will lead him home.
So what's the point of mourning as I do?
Now that I've seen my city, Ilium,
fare as it fared and those who captured it
being judged at last by gods, as happens here,
I'll also go inside and face my death.   1290
You see these doors? I call them Hades' gates.
My only prayer is this: one fatal blow.
I won't resist. I'll calmly close my eyes
and let my vital blood all flow away.

CORYPHAEUS:
How very sorrowful and wise you are!
You've said a lot; but if you've truly seen
your death, then why walk down this deadly path
serenely, like a sacrificial ox?

CASSANDRA:
Since no evasion's possible, my friends.

CORYPHAEUS:
One's final moments have the greatest worth.   1300

CASSANDRA:
The day is here and little gained by flight.

CORYPHAEUS:
You're stout of heart, enduring as you do.

CASSANDRA:
That's praise that happy people rarely hear!

CORYPHAEUS:
To die with dignity's a blessing, though.

CASSANDRA (walking toward the palace):
O father dear, your noble sons and you!

(CASSANDRA stops abruptly and twists away.)

CORYPHAEUS:
What happened there? What turned you back in horror?

CASSANDRA:
Pheu! Pheu!

CORYPHAEUS:
What's that? You must imagine something foul.

CASSANDRA:
This house. It reeks of bloody massacres.

CORYPHAEUS:
I only smell the hearthside sacrifice.   1310

CASSANDRA:
The stench is very like an open grave's.

CORYPHAEUS:
They're burning incense there, but that's not it.

CASSANDRA:
I'll enter anyway and there bewail
my fate and Agamemnon's. Life is done.
Oh my friends!
I'm not a timid bird who flies away
from every bush. Please say so when I die,
and when another woman dies for me,
another man for that ill-mated man.
As death draws near, I seek that friendly boon.   1320

CORYPHAEUS:
Poor girl, I pity your appointed doom!

CASSANDRA:
I have some parting words—a dirge, if you
prefer. Before this blazing sun, my last,
I pray my lord's avengers also take
his enemies to task for killing me,
the easy crime of murdering a slave.
Alas for men's affairs! When fortune smiles,
they're merely shades, and when misfortune comes,
a moistened sponge erases everything.
I pity mankind even more than me.   1330

        (Exit CASSANDRA into the palace.)

CHORUS:
No mortal imagines he's had   Anapests (1331–1342)
an adequate run of success,
and waves it away from his mansion,
exclaiming, "Don't ever come back!"
The blessed immortals permitted
Agamemnon to subjugate Troy.
He's back in his home with their blessing.
But what if the Fates make him pay

for the blood that his ancestors shed?
And what if by dying he causes
the dead to exact other deaths?
Would anyone hearing that story
see nothing to fear in their fate?

AGAMEMNON (inside the palace):
Omoi! I'm struck a mortal blow within!   1343

CORYPHAEUS:
Quiet! Who's that shouting that he's struck a mortal
      blow?

AGAMEMNON:
Omoi! I'm struck again, a second time!

CORYPHAEUS:
Judging by our ruler's cries, the deed we feared is done.
Let's consider what the prudent way to act would be.

CHORISTER 1:
I'll tell you my proposal. Rally all
the citizens to swarm the palace now!

CHORISTER 2:
I think we'd better rush them right away   1350
and catch the killers holding bloody swords.

CHORISTER 3:
I say that your opinion's right. I vote
to act. There isn't time to hesitate.

CHORISTER 4:
The way that they're beginning makes it clear.
The signs are there. They're planning tyranny!

CHORISTER 5:
We're wasting time. Meanwhile their sleepless acts
cast mud on circumspection's good repute.

CHORISTER 6:
I haven't any plan to recommend.
To act, however, does demand a plan.

CHORISTER 7:
And I agree. It isn't possible   1360
to resurrect a murdered man with words.

CHORISTER 8:
Shall we prolong our lives by giving way
to leaders who degrade the royal house?

CHORISTER 9:
No! That's unbearable. I'd rather die;
for death's a kinder fate than tyranny.

CHORISTER 10:
Can we infer the man is truly dead
from hearing him exclaim, *"Omoi! Omoi!"*?

CHORISTER 11:
Our situation calls for certainty.
To guess and know precisely aren't the same.

CORYPHAEUS:
I gather everyone agrees with that.   1370
We need the king's condition clarified.

> (The palace doors open, revealing CLYTAEMESTRA
> holding a sword over the dead bodies of AGAMEMNON
> and CASSANDRA.)

CLYTAEMESTRA:

I uttered many useful words before,
which I won't blush at contradicting now.
How else could anyone preparing war
against apparent friends encircle them
with nets of grief they couldn't overleap?
This final round of ancient strife was planned
by me for many years. It took some time.
I'm standing where I struck, my work complete.
I won't deny my methods guaranteed   1380
he wouldn't have a chance to fight or flee.
I threw an endless fishing net around
his head and arms, an evil wealth of clothes,
and struck him twice. Each time he shouted, "*O!*"
then loosed his limbs. I struck another blow,
a third, when he had fallen, pious thanks
to chthonic Zeus,[81] who guards the dead below.
He lay there wheezing life away. At last,
he vomited a shining clot of blood,
which dappled me with dark red drops of dew.   1390
It made me glad, as glad as farmers' fields
when thanks to god the blossoms start to bloom.
So matters stand, my honored elders here.
Rejoice or don't, but I'll say thankful prayers.

(CLYTAEMESTRA pauses to look at AGAMEMNON's
wounds.)

If corpses had libations poured on them,
this blood would be the perfect offering.
He filled our mixing bowl with monstrous crimes.
Returning here, he had to drain it dry.

81. Hades.

CORYPHAEUS:
Your words have left us speechless. You're so bold!
To boast like that above a fallen man!   1400

CLYTAEMESTRA:
You think that I'm a foolish woman, eh?
I feel no trepidation, saying things
that you already know. Your praise and blame
mean nothing. Agamemnon's lying here,
my husband, now a corpse, my handiwork,
completely justified, and that is that.

CHORUS:
What evil food or drink produced   Strophe 1 (1407–1411)
    on earth or flowing sea
did you consume to undertake
    this awful butchery?

The people curse you for your act.
    You've severed all your ties.
You'll be a homeless outcast now,
    whom citizens despise.

CLYTAEMESTRA:
So now you'd vote to banish me. You say   1412
I'm hated, cursed by all the citizens;
and yet you didn't criticize this man
who sacrificed his daughter like a lamb
his teeming wooly flocks would never miss,
the dearest child my labor pains brought forth,
slain as a charm to calm the Thracian winds.
Well? Shouldn't you have banished him for such
an action? Judging me, you suddenly   1420
become indignant. Go! Go utter threats

while understanding this: I'm well prepared
for you to rule—if you can conquer me
by force. If god has something else in mind,
you'll learn to practice prudence late in life.

CHORUS:
Your plans are grand. Your words are loud Antistrophe 1 (1426–1430)
    and full of arrogance.
As though made mad by spilling blood,
    you're lost to common sense.

You can't conceal your bloodshot eyes.
    Some day, deprived of friends,
you'll pay for every bloody blow.
    You'll have to make amends.

CLYTAEMESTRA:
You'd better hear this other oath of mine.   1431
By Justice, which my daughter has at last,
by Curse[82] and Ruin, my accomplices,
no fear will come tiptoeing overhead
while in my hearth the fire's kindled by
Aegisthus, loyal past and present friend,
the ample shield my courage stands behind.

    (Gesturing toward AGAMEMNON.)

Here lies the husband who abused me so,
the slave girls' darling under Trojan walls;

    (Toward CASSANDRA.)

82. The Greek word here is *Erinys*, meaning primarily a Fury but also a
curse personified.

and there the prophet taken prisoner,   1440
the concubine who spouted oracles,
his wife, who knew the sailors' benches well
and rubbed their masts.[83] They've gotten their reward.
He simply died, while she—she warbled like
a swan who sings a final mournful song.
She was his lover. Now she's given me
a tasty bit of bedroom pleasure too.[84]

CHORUS:
Come quickly, death—less lingering   Strophe 2 (1448–1454)
  disease and wrenching pain.
We need the endless rest you bring.
    Our kindly guard's been slain.
One woman made his lifetime grim.
Another woman murdered him.

Eeoo! What insanity, Helen!   Anapests (1455–1467)
A woman alone, you destroyed
so many—incredibly many!—
brave soldiers who fought under Troy.
And now you have added a final
memorial bloom to your wreath

83. An obscenity unparalleled in extant Greek tragedies. The meaning seems transparent. The same image occurs in Strabo 8.6.20. Fraenkel's commentary on the play (p. 683) describes the critical word, *histotribēs* (mast-rubber), as "completely obscure"! See Sommerstein, "Comic Elements in Tragic Language."

84. Another shocking remark that some editors have changed. The implication of the text as it stands is that Clytaemestra was sexually aroused by killing Cassandra. Skeptical editors argue that the word for bed in Greek, *eunēs*, is an interpolation that displaced some adjective that left the nature of Clytaemestra's additional pleasure unspecified.

by shedding indelible blood.
A murderous Fury has surely
brought grief to the men of your house.

CLYTAEMESTRA:
Don't ask for immediate death,
because of the weight of these things.
Don't heap indignation on Helen
as bringing destruction to men,
as costing the Danaans[85] lives,
and causing unbearable pain.

CHORUS:
The god attacking Tantalids[86]   Antistrophe 2 (1468–1474)
   employs a matching pair
of women doing as he bids.
   It's more than I can bear.
See! On the corpse, the hateful crow
sings tuneless hymns to gods below!

CLYTAEMESTRA:
At last you've corrected your language   Anapests (1475–1480)
by naming our family fiend,
the triply surfeited demon
who fosters our bloodthirsty lust.
Before the old agony ceases,
fresh ichor is destined to flow.

85. Another name for the Greeks.
86. The descendants of Tantalus (tan´-tə´-lis), the mythical figure who was the supposed father of Pelops and thus the grandfather of Atreus and Thyestes and the great-grandfather of Agamemnon and Aegisthus. See Appendix 3, "The *Oresteia* and Myth."

SEMI-CHORUS 1:

You say there's a Fury besieging your house,[87]   Strophe 3 (1481–1488)
a demon so angry and great
that its thirst for misfortune can never be quenched.
What a horrible tale to relate!

SEMI-CHORUS 2:

Ee-oo! Ee-ay! It's the working of Zeus.
He's everything's agent and cause.
What mortal event's not accomplished by him?
Even this is approved by his laws.

CHORUS:

My king, teach me how to lament!   Anapests (1489–1504)
What words will express my devotion?
You lie in this spider web dying,
exhaling the last of your life.
An impious murder! Ungodly!
A resting place fit for a slave!
Done in by a treacherous fate
and a wife with a double-edged sword.

CLYTAEMESTRA:

You claim that the murder was mine?
Not so! You're mistaken to think
that I'm Agamemnon's real wife.
An ancient embittered avenger,
who mimicked the spouse of this corpse,
exacted the price for the wretched

87. My division of this choral song into separate performances by semi-choruses is based on the content of the song. In both strophe and antistrophe, the second four lines sound like a corrective to the first four.

banquet that Atreus gave.
The blood of a full-grown adult
has paid for the death of the young.

SEMI-CHORUS 1:

Is anyone likely to testify that   Antistrophe 3 (1505–1512)
    you are not to be blamed for this deed,
though a demon avenging his father's offense
    may also have helped you succeed?

SEMI-CHORUS 2:

Black Ares advances on rivers of blood.
    When kinsmen are slain he'll intrude.
He'd have gone anywhere to gain justice for those
    little children being treated as food.

CHORUS:

My king, teach me how to lament.   Anapests (1513–1529)
What words will express my devotion?
You lie in this spider web dying,
exhaling the last of your life.
An impious murder! Ungodly!
A resting place fit for a slave!
Done in by a treacherous fate
and a wife with a double-edged sword.

CLYTAEMESTRA:

My opinion is different. I'd say
that he died in a suitable manner.
His treachery ruined our house.
He murdered our offspring, our darling,
our Iphigenia.
His sufferings balanced his deeds.

He won't be so boastful in Hades.[88]
He died by the sword for his sins.

CHORUS:
Where to turn? I'm at a loss,   Strophe 4 (1530–1536)
    although I wrack my brain.
The house is falling. Thunder blasts
    foretell a bloody rain.
One shower stops, but Fate now hones
    its instruments of pain
on new whetstones to use once more
    as Justice shall ordain.

If only you'd swallowed me, Earth,   Anapests (1537–1559)
before I had witnessed this sight,
this man in a basin of silver
that serves as his deathbed, alas!
Who's willing to bury this man?
Who's ready to sing a lament?

            (Addressing CLYTAEMESTRA.)

And you? Would you dare to start mourning
your victim—your husband, no less?
You'd render his spirit a service
in thanks for the great things he's done,
but it wouldn't be pleasing or just.
Who'll offer a graveside oration
for someone so nearly divine?
Who'll do so while weeping sincerely?

---

88. Possibly an allusion to the two appearances of Agamemnon's ghost
in Homer's *Odyssey* (11.405–434; 24.19–97). Far from boasting, his main
theme is the pitiable nature of his death.

CLYTAEMESTRA:
You needn't attend to his rites.
We killed him. We'll bury him too,
but not amid outsiders' dirges,
for Iphigenia, his daughter,
will welcome him, standing beside
the swift-flowing river of grief.[89]
She'll hug him and give him a kiss.

CHORUS:
Insults are flying thick and fast. Antistrophe 4 (1560–1566)
    The truth remains unknown,
but plunderers are plundered too;
    and killers must atone.
Who acts must suffer. That's the law
    while Zeus sits on his throne.
This household's glued to Ruin. Who
    will save this curséd home?

CLYTAEMESTRA:
You hit on a truth in that oracle! Anapests (1567–1576)
I willingly promise the demon
of Pleisthenid vengeance[90] to be
contented with things as they are,
hard to endure though they be,

---

89. A reference to the Acheron, an underworld river. A Greek word for grief is *achos*.

90. While Homer describes Atreus as the father of Agamemnon and Menelaus, scholia to the *Iliad* report that according to Hesiod they were sons of a certain Pleisthenes. When he died, Agamemnon and Menelaus were adopted by their grandfather, Atreus. Aeschylus, however, describes Agamemnon and Menelaus as children of Atreus (*Agamemnon* 60). It is likely that here and at 1602 he thought of "Pleisthenes" as just another name for Atreus.

if leaving this house he will vex
others with murders by kin.
A moderate fortune's sufficient,
provided reciprocal slaughter
and madness are gone from my halls.

(Enter AEGISTHUS from the palace with several
SOLDIERS.)

AEGISTHUS:
Ah, friendly light of justice-bringing day!   1577
At last I'd say that gods watch over men
and see their sorrows high above the earth.
This sight convinces me, this man who lies   1580
trapped in a Furies' web to pay for crimes
his father's hand committed. Lovely sight!
His father, Atreus, once ruled this land,
but rivals challenged him—specifically,
a brother named Thyestes. (I'm his son.)
Atreus banished him from house and town;
but he came back, this poor Thyestes did,
a hearthside suppliant, and gained this pledge:
he'd never spill his blood on native ground.
Then this man's father, godless Atreus,   1590
with passion born of anything but love,
pretended he'd prepared a friendly meal
and fed my father children's flesh instead,
excluding feet and rakes that end the arms.[91]
Seated apart, Thyestes couldn't tell.

91. The "rakes" are fingers, excluded because they would be instantly
recognized as human. Since the victims' heads would also have to be concealed,
it is possible that a line mentioning them has been lost.

Accepting some, he ate it, lethal food,
as you can see, for this entire house.
Next, when he understood his awful act,
he wailed, fell back, and coughed the carnage up.
"May painful deaths pursue Pelopidae!"[92]   1600
he prayed and kicked the table, adding this:
"So perish all the race of Pleisthenes!"
That's why this person died before your eyes,
and I was right to plan the bloody deed.
I was my father's third-born child, a babe
in swaddling clothes, exiled by Atreus,
but Justice brought me back full-grown,
and *I* caught *him*. I waited by the gates,
it's true, but all the clever plans were mine.
Now that I've seen this scoundrel caught in nets   1610
that Justice wove, I'll die a happy man.

CORYPHAEUS:
Aegisthus, boasting's wrong in troubled times.
You say you freely killed this man; at least,
you planned his ghastly murder by yourself.
I say that Justice must be done. Be warned!
You won't escape the people's rock-hard curse.

AEGISTHUS:
I hear your voices coming from below.
Real power occupies the upper decks.
You'll find obedience is rather hard
to learn, old man, when someone's old as you.   1620
However, prison, age, and hunger pangs

___

92. Pelopidae (pe-lŏ´-pi-dī) are descendants of Pelops, the son of Tantalus
and father of Atreus and Thyestes.

make excellent instructors, mystic priests,
and healers. Having eyes, you must see this.
By kicking goads, you only hurt yourself.

CORYPHAEUS:
Woman! You stayed at home awaiting men's
return from battle, shamed a husband's bed
with lust, and planned our manly leader's death!

AEGISTHUS:
With words like those you're sowing bitter tears.
You really are an anti-Orpheus!
His joyous voice led everything to him;[93]   1630
your irritating noise will lead to jail,
but there you'll learn to sing a nicer song.

CORYPHAEUS:
As though you'll be the Argives' ruler, you
who planned this homicide but didn't have
the fortitude to murder him yourself!

AEGISTHUS:
The ambush was, of course, the woman's job.
No one would trust an ancient foe like me.
I mean to use his ample wealth to rule.
If someone proves recalcitrant, his neck
will feel a heavy yoke. He won't be like   1640
a sleek racehorse well-fed. No! hunger pangs
and dark will watch him growing nice and soft.

93. The songs of the legendary musician Orpheus (ȯr´-fē-əs) were so
enchanting that trees and wild animals gathered around him to listen.

CORYPHAEUS:
Why didn't you, you coward, murder him
yourself? Why have the woman kill the man
and so pollute the land and native gods?
Does good Orestes see the light somewhere?
May kindly fate return him here to be
this pair's triumphant executioner!

AEGISTHUS:
Since you choose such words and actions, you'll be
    educated first.

(Addressing his SOLDIERS.)

Pay attention, fellow soldiers! Here is work for you
    to do!   1650

CAPTAIN OF THE GUARDS:
Pay attention, everybody! Be prepared to draw your
    swords.

CORYPHAEUS:
I'm prepared to draw my weapon! What is more, to
    fight and die.

AEGISTHUS:
"Die?" Your word! I like that omen! Let what's fated
    come to pass!

CLYTAEMESTRA (addressing AEGISTHUS):
Not like that, my dearest lover. Please refrain from
    further ills.
Those that we have reaped already make a grievous
    summer's crop.

Pain enough has been inflicted. Let the bloodshed
    finally stop.

(Addressing the CHORUS.)

Seek your houses, honored elders, yielding to necessity,
lest you suffer some misfortune. Things we did just had
    to be.
If some end of toil and trouble does appear, we won't
    resist.
We're exhausted, beaten bloody by a demon's iron fist.   1660
That's a woman's understanding, if there's anyone who
    cares.

AEGISTHUS:
Shall these fools go right on plucking blossoms from
    their useless tongues,
blithely tempting fate by using words designed to give
    offense?
Those who rail against their masters sorely lack in
    common sense!

CORYPHAEUS:
This is not an Argive custom: flattering the cowardly.

AEGISTHUS:
In the future I'll be keeping eyes on everything you do.

CORYPHAEUS:
Not if heaven helps Orestes find a way of coming back!

AEGISTHUS:
Exiles eagerly devour empty hopes. How well I know!

CORYPHAEUS:
Keep it up! Get fat polluting Justice, while you have the
    chance.

AEGISTHUS:
Be forewarned: don't be so stupid! There's a heavy price
    to pay. 1670

CORYPHAEUS:
Keep on boasting like a rooster showing off beside his hen.

CLYTAEMESTRA (addressing AEGISTHUS):
Just ignore their harmless snarling. We have work to do
    inside,
taking care of household matters in a way that's dignified.

    (CLYTAEMESTRA walks purposefully into the palace.
    AEGISTHUS lingers briefly to glare at the departing
    elders. His SOLDIERS hurry them out of the area along
    a parodos.)

Libation Bearers

Characters

ORESTES, son of Agamemnon and Clytaemestra
PYLADES, Orestes' companion, son of Orestes' guardian,
    Strophius of Phocis
CHORUS, elderly serving women
CORYPHAEUS, the leader of the chorus
ELECTRA, Orestes' sister
DOORMAN, a palace servant
CLYTAEMESTRA, Orestes' mother
CLYTAEMESTRA'S ATTENDANT
CILISSA, an elderly servant, the infant Orestes' nurse
AEGISTHUS, Clytaemestra's lover
SERVANTS

(Like *Agamemnon*, this play is set before Agamemnon's
palace. A stone slab in the foreground marks his grave,
the focal point of the action during the first half of
the play. Thereafter attention shifts to the palace itself and its main entrance doors. There is a statue of
Hermes beside the entrance to the palace. ORESTES
and PYLADES enter from a parodos and stand by the
tomb. ORESTES' hair is braided. He holds a sheared
lock in his hand.)

ORESTES:

Hermes, who rules the lower world and guards[1]   1
my father's powers, be my ally! Be
my savior! Hear my prayer. I've come. I've reached   3
[my native land, in search of just revenge]
for one who died by violent female hands,   3a
done in by surreptitious treachery.   3b
[Arriving here, I sacrificed] a lock
of hair to Inachus[2] for raising me,   6
and now I'll place a second mournful lock   7
here on the grave in which my father lies   4
and also call on him to hear and heed.   5
Father, I wasn't here to mourn your death   8
or bid farewell as your procession passed.   9

(ORESTES stops abruptly, hearing the CHORUS of
elderly slave women approach.)

What's this I see? What female company   10
approaches, all decked out in pitch-black robes?
There's some misfortune driving them, but what?
Has some new sorrow touched our family?
Or do these women bring my father gifts,

1. The beginning of *Libation Bearers* is missing from the single manuscript
on which our texts depend. Eleven lines preserved as quotations in other works
are used by editors to reconstruct the prologue. The version printed here
follows Alan Sommerstein's edition of the *Oresteia*, with slight alterations of
my own.

2. Inachus (i´-nə-kəs), a small river near Argos and also therefore a river
god.

libations meant to pacify the dead?
That's surely it. I see my sister there,
Electra, drawing near, conspicuous
in grief. Let me avenge my father's death,
O Zeus! Become my willing comrade now!
Come, Pylades, let's back away and learn   20
more clearly what this supplication means.

> (ORESTES and PYLADES conceal themselves by return-
> ing to the parodos. Led by ELECTRA, the CHORUS
> comes out of the palace and assumes positions in the
> orchēstra facing Agamemnon's tomb. Each CHORISTER
> carries a jar.)

CHORUS:

We left the house as ordered,   Strophe 1 (22–31)
   a libation-bearing throng.
The sound of flesh being beaten
   accentuates our song.
Our cheeks are red from scratching
   with bloody fingernails.
Our hearts must always pasture
   where someone weeps and wails.
One hears the linen ripping,
   the rending of our gowns,
and folds across our bosoms,
   struck when Fortune frowns.

The house's hair is bristling   Antistrophe 1 (32–41)
   because an angry dream,
which seemed all too prophetic,
   provoked a midnight scream,
like enemies invading
   where womenfolk recline.

The apparition experts
*   declared the dream divine.*
Some under ground, they stated,
*   are feeling sorely tried.*
Their deadly wrath's directed
*   at those by whom they died.*

Sweet mother Earth, the gods must hate   Strophe 2 (42–53)
the eager wife who sent me here,
to turn away her evil fate
with courtesies that aren't sincere.

I fear to ask the following:
when blood is spilled and soaks the plain,
have men discovered anything
that washes off the ugly stain?

The hearth is wretched. Grief upends
the house. The sun has left the sky.
The darkness all men hate descends
on homes when masters die.

Once Reverence never knew defeat;   Antistrophe 2 (54–65)
it pierced the public ear and heart,
a power one could not unseat,
but now it's standing far apart.

Fears are ever-wider spread.
Success is now a god and more.
But Justice watches overhead.
She holds the scales and keeps the score.

She deals with some at once by day.
In other cases pains don't come

till twilight does, and then they pay,
and midnight handles some.

Revenge congeals when bloodshed blends   Strophe 3 (66–70)
with fertile soil. Then ruin rends
the guilty man. It never ends.

As there's no cure for maid profaned,   Antistrophe 3 (71–75)
so every stream would wash a stained,
polluted killer's hands in vain.

Since gods ordained my city's fall,   Epode (74–83)
enslaving me, I celebrate
my rulers' actions, one and all—
those just, those not—and stifle hate.

My veils conceal my secret pain.
I mourn for kings who died in vain.
I'm numb with hidden grief.

ELECTRA:
My serving women, household managers,   84
since you're attending these solemnities,
be my advisors. Tell me this. What words
are right while pouring these sepulchral gifts?
What gracious prayer would Father like to hear?
Should I maintain that Mother's gifts are from
"a loving wife for her beloved man"?   90
Or what about a normal prayer like this?
"Repay the persons sending you these gifts
with all the kindness . . . evil deeds deserve!"
Or should I come in silence, shamefully,
as Father died, and spill this fluid, make
a muddy stream, like someone emptying

a common jar without a backward glance?
I'm not so bold. There's nothing I can say
that fits this offering on Father's grave.
Take part with me in these reflections, friends.   100
We have a common enemy at home.
Don't hide your inward feelings out of fear.
One destined end awaits us all, the free
and those enslaved by someone else's hand.
If you've some better counsel, let me know!

CORYPHAEUS:
Your father's tomb's a holy place for me.
I'll speak my honest thought as you command.

ELECTRA:
Do so, in keeping with your reverence!

CORYPHAEUS:
Pray as you pour that Fortune aid "true friends."

ELECTRA:
Who are the friends that you'd entitle "true"?   110

CORYPHAEUS:
First you, then all who hate Aegisthus next.

ELECTRA:
In other words, I pray for me and you?

CORYPHAEUS:
I'll leave that up to you to figure out.

ELECTRA:
And should I add another to the group?

CORYPHAEUS:
Why, yes! Orestes, though he's far away.

ELECTRA:
Well said! That isn't bad advice at all.

CORYPHAEUS:
Mention the murder next and those to blame.

ELECTRA:
I need your guidance. Tell me what to say.

CORYPHAEUS:
Pray that some god or mortal man arrives.

ELECTRA:
To judge the murderers or punish them?   120

CORYPHAEUS:
Just say: for deadly reciprocity.

ELECTRA:
Is that a pious thing to ask of gods?

CORYPHAEUS:
Avenging injuries with evils? Yes!   123

ELECTRA (praying):
Lord Hermes, greatest herald, messenger[3]   165

3. Line 165 was probably omitted by mistake in the course of the manuscript tradition and then restored to the wrong position after line 164. Modern editors print it here, after line 123, where it fits well.

of higher gods and lower ones, be mine.   124
Instruct the ghosts of my ancestral home,
who dwell beneath the earth, and Mother Earth
herself, who bears all things and nurses them,
then takes her offspring back, to hear my prayers
while I dispense these lustral offerings,
praying to my father thus: O pity me!   130
And let Orestes light our house once more!
We might as well be servants sold abroad.
Our mother traded us and got a man,
Aegisthus—her assistant murderer.
I dwell in servitude, Orestes strays,
deprived of property that's rightly his,
and they exult in wealth your labors earned.
I pray the fated turns his journeys take
restore Orestes. Father, hear! For me,
I only ask to be more virtuous   140
than Mother was and act more righteously.
That prayer's for us. Regarding enemies,
father, I pray that your avenger comes
and that your killers die as they deserve.
I hide those words inside this friendly prayer.
An evil curse is all I have for them.
Arise! Bring noble gifts and allied gods,
bring Earth and Justice, source of victory.
To end my prayers, I'll pour libations now.

> (ELECTRA addresses the CHORUS, then pours liba-
> tions on her father's tomb while the CHORUS performs
> a brief song.)

The custom is for you to ornament   150
the rite with mournful hymns that praise the dead.

CHORUS:
Shed splashing tears, the master's dead. Choral Interlude (152–163)
He guarded well the good and true,
for all the evil things we dread
were healed by him or else withdrew.

Now that libations soak the ground,
O lord and master down below,
hear my heart's unhappy sound:
O-O! O-O! O-Toi! Eeoo!

O set us free, some great warlord!
Wield weapons from your northern land,
the bows, the darts, the hilted sword
for use in fighting hand-to-hand.

ELECTRA:
Since Father has his muddy offerings now,   164
I'd like to share another bit of news.   166

CORYPHAEUS:
Do tell. My heart's begun a fearful dance.

ELECTRA:
There's hair atop the tomb, a curly lock.

CORYPHAEUS:
Some man's? Or is a buxom maid the source?

ELECTRA:
The answer's obvious to everyone.   170

CORYPHAEUS:
And might an older woman learn from youth?

ELECTRA:
Nobody could have cut it off but me.

CORYPHAEUS:
His other relatives are enemies.[4]

ELECTRA:
Besides, the hair looks very similar . . .

CORYPHAEUS:
To whose? Speak up! We really want to know.

ELECTRA:
It bears a strong resemblance to my own.[5]

CORYPHAEUS:
Is it a secret gift Orestes left?

ELECTRA:
The hair *is* very similar to his.

4. Only relatives were likely to dedicate locks of hair at gravesites. The coryphaeus means that Clytaemestra is the only other possible source, and she is too hostile to have sacrificed a lock of her hair.

5. Euripides' *Electra* 513–546 ridicules the evidence that suggests Orestes' presence to Aeschylus' Electra. An elderly servant points out the absurdity of assuming that brother and sister would have identical locks of hair, to say nothing of identical footprints, or that Orestes would still be wearing a cloak that Electra wove for him as a child. Some commentators try to make sense of Electra's suppositions, arguing, for example, that the footprints involved were identical in proportion, not size. I prefer to think that Aeschylus' toleration of the irrational is an aspect of his authorial persona. I discuss this point in my introduction.

CORYPHAEUS:
Then did he dare to make the journey here?

ELECTRA:
He merely sent the lock for father's sake.   180

CORYPHAEUS:
That explanation leaves me sad. It means
his feet will never touch this land again.

ELECTRA:
A tidal wave of worry likewise washed
across my heart. A piercing arrow struck,
transfixing me, and ceaseless, desperate tears
fall from my eyes like violent winter rains.
But since I've seen these braided strands, can I
believe they're just some stranger's offering?
And yet the killer didn't dedicate
her hair. I mean my "mother," as she's called.   190
The title doesn't suit her godless heart.
Well, then, dare I approve my other thought?
Perhaps the dearest man of all, Orestes, left
this gift, but no! That's Hope deluding me.
Phay-oo!
If only hair could talk and reason like
a messenger, I wouldn't waver so.
I'd either learn to hate this twisted lock
because a hostile head provided it,
or it could weep with me, a kindred soul,
honor my father, decorate his tomb.   200
But look! Another piece of evidence!⁶   205

6. Following the suggestion in Oliver Taplin, *The Stagecraft of Aeschylus: The Dramatic Use of Exits and Entrances in Greek Tragedy*, 337–38, I have

Footprints! Alike, resembling mine! No, wait!
I see two pairs of feet in outline now—
beside the man's, some fellow traveler's.
I'll measure one.

(She places one of her feet on top of a footprint on the
ground.)

         The heel and tendons both
leave traces matching perfectly with mine!   210
What agony I feel! I'm going mad!
The gods to whom we pray know very well   201
the violent storms by which we mariners   202
are tossed, but if we're fated to survive,   203
a little seed could grow a giant tree.   204

(ORESTES steps forward from his hiding place.)

ORESTES:
Declare that gods have answered all your prayers
and pray they do the same for future ones!

(ELECTRA reacts to ORESTES' sudden appearance in
a strangely calm manner, as if it was expected.)

ELECTRA:
Why? What's the favor gods have granted me?

ORESTES:
Meeting with him you've often prayed to see.

---

transposed lines 201–204 to follow 211. The initial exchanges between Orestes
and Electra flow more naturally in this way.

ELECTRA:
And who's this mortal man I've prayed to see?

ORESTES:
I've often heard you sing Orestes' praise.

ELECTRA:
But what has that to do with answered prayers?

ORESTES:
I'm he! You'll never find a better friend.

ELECTRA:
Please don't entangle me in some deceit!   220

ORESTES (smiling):
You think I'm weaving plots against myself?

ELECTRA:
You dare to laugh at my misfortunes now?

ORESTES:
If so, I'm mocking mine, since they're the same.

ELECTRA:
Should I be calling you Orestes then?

ORESTES:
You're slow to recognize me face-to-face,
but when you saw a mourner's lock of hair
and matched the tracks your footfalls left with mine,[7]   228

---

7. Lines 227–228 and 229–230 were transposed by earlier editors, a decision followed by Sommerstein.

your heart took flight. Those things persuaded you.   227
Restore that hair to its position.   230

> (He holds the lock against his own head, where some
> hair is missing.)

Look!

Your brother's hair, and not unlike your own!   229
Look at my cloak! The weaving's yours! You stroked
the loom. You wove this frightening animal.

> (ELECTRA reacts joyously. She and ORESTES embrace.)

Be still, however. Don't go mad with joy.
Beware! Those nearest us are bitter foes!

ELECTRA:
O dearest treasure Father's house still owns!
O tear-stained hope of better things to come!
Take heart and win your patrimony back!
O four-times-precious light! For I'm compelled
to call you Father now, and I direct
three other loves your way: the love   240
I had for Mother, whom I justly hate;
love for my sister, cruelly sacrificed;
and you, my loyal brother, pride and joy.
I only pray that Justice, Force, and Zeus,
the third and greatest, stand beside you now.

ORESTES (praying):
Observe our circumstances, lord god Zeus!
Behold the eagle father's lonesome brood,
their sire dead in evil twists and coils,
a fearsome viper's trap. Starvation racks

the orphaned chicks. They're immature. They can't   250
bring home the kind of spoil their father did.
As you can see, Electra here and I
are like the eaglets, orphaned progeny,
and both exiled, deprived of rightful homes.
Recall our father's sacrifices, how
they honored you. If you permit his chicks
to perish, where will you obtain the like?
The signs you send to mortal men will cease
to be believed. Come festive days, no ox
will grace your altar, once this royal tree   260
withers and dies completely, root and branch.
Protect us! You can make a little house
a palace, fallen though it seems to be.

CORYPHAEUS:
O children, you who've saved your father's hearth,
be quiet, youngsters, lest somebody hear
and mention all these things in idle talk
to those in power—those I'd like to see
covered in pitch and fatal flames some day!

ORESTES:
The mighty oracle of Loxias,
which ordered me to take this risk, will not   270
betray me. He declared in piercing tones
that constant storms would freeze my rebel heart
unless I sought my father's murderers
and murdered them in turn the selfsame way.
As penalty for failure he declared
I'd be destroyed by wrenching illnesses
and sanctions worse than loss of property.
He spoke of anger felt toward living men
by those below. He cited dread disease,

ulcers attacking flesh with hungry jaws,   280
malignant sores corroding healthy skin,
albino hair that sprouts where illness lies.
He mentioned other things: the punishments
that Furies born of fathers' blood inflict,   284
the unseen bolt that's hurled by those beneath[8]   286
the ground, the fallen, vengeance-seeking kin.
Then madness comes with nighttime's false alarms.
One's rousted, dazed, and driven out of town.
His body's scarred by whips with metal prongs.   290
He can't enjoy communal mixing bowls,
partake in streams from which libations flow.
No altar's safe. His father's wrath is there
unseen. Nobody shares his bed and board.
In time he dies dishonored, loved by none,
a shriveled corpse done in by lethal fate.
Who'd disregard prophetic words like those?
But even if I did, there's work to do.
For many motives merge: the god's commands,
my father's bitter grief, the loss besides   300
of my estate. That too distresses me.
A pair of women shouldn't dominate
those most distinguished citizens, those men
whose celebrated spirit conquered Troy.
That's right. I said *two* women. Time will tell.

CHORUS:
Great Fates by appointment of Zeus,   Anapests (306–314)
we seek a conclusion,
the resting place Justice is straining to reach;
for Justice cries out that a debt must be paid.

8. Line 285 is deleted by most editors, since it cannot be made to fit
syntactically: "one seeing (someone) raising his bright brows in the darkness."

Let speech that is hateful be answered by hate,
and murderous blows pay a murderous price.
The words of antiquity ring in our ears:
the doer must suffer the deed.[9]

ORESTES:
Unhappy father, tell me what Strophe 1 (315–322)
    I need to do or say
to reach your final resting place.
    You lie so far away.

The worlds of light and dark diverge,
    but eulogies are said
to please the Atreids who lie
    out here among the dead.

CHORUS:
The fire's hungry jaw, my son, Strophe 2 (324–331)
does not destroy the dead man's will.
He shows his anger later on.
He's dead and mourned but dangerous still.

The wild, emotional laments
occasioned by the homicide
of fathers and begetters rouse
just avengers far and wide.

ELECTRA:
O Father, hear our sorrows now, Antistrophe 1 (332–339)
    see tears that flood our eyes,
two children visiting your grave,

9. Rather than saying that we should do unto others as we would have others do unto us, the chorus cautions that others will in fact treat us as we treat them; hence, we will suffer the same injuries that we inflict.

bewailing your demise.
We're fugitives and suppliants
your grave has taken in.
What good is here? What evil's not?
When doesn't Ruin win?

CHORUS:
If god so desires, perhaps, he'll transform   Anapests (340–344)
your voices to music more cheerful by far.
Instead of laments at the side of a tomb,
a paean may rattle the palace's roof
to welcome a bowl of new wine.

ORESTES:
I wish that you'd been slain by some   Strophe 3 (345–353)
Lycian[10] *spear at Ilium,*
Father, not at home.

You would have left a house renowned,
and when we children walked around,
we'd turn heads everywhere.

Abroad a lofty monument
would mark your grave, not represent
the shame our house must bear.

CHORUS:
A friend to friends who died at Troy,   Antistrophe 2 (354–362)
illustrious beneath the earth,
an honored lord attending on
the chthonic kings of greatest worth—

10. Lycia (lǐ´-shē-ə; adj. lǐ-shē´-ən), a region in southern Asia Minor. Lycians, notably the hero Sarpedon, fought in the Trojan War on the Trojan side.

indeed, he was a king himself
as long as he drew mortal breath.
A royal scepter made of him
an arbiter of life and death.

ELECTRA:
I'd not have wished for you to fall,   Antistrophe 3 (363–371)
dear Father, by the Trojan wall,
buried with the rest,

the host that Trojan spears laid low
beside Scamander's stream. Oh no!
I'd want your killers slain,

so even people far away
and not involved would have to say
they knew their deadly end.

CHORUS:
Such blessings, my daughter, are better than   Anapests (372–379)
        gold.
They're better than great, mythological luck.
You speak of them. Yes. But that's all you can do.
Two lashes are landing with thuds on your back.
Those who'd protect you are under the ground,
while persons in power have blood on their hands.
Of all the indignities you must endure,
is any more hateful than that?[11]

11. A conjectural restoration of the closing sentiment. Some words have
been omitted in the manuscript. Translated literally, the remaining words
are: "of those hateful . . . but to children . . . more . . . has been."

ORESTES:

That stabs my ear! By Zeus who sends　　　　Strophe 4 (380–385)
the fury Ruin from below,
so reckless villains make amends
with punishment that's sure but slow,
parental debts will all be paid!

CHORUS:

A man struck down, a woman dead,　　　　Strophe 5 (386–392)
that's what I want to celebrate.
Why keep the thought inside my head?
My heart's a windstorm full of hate.

ELECTRA:

Oh when will Zeus, almighty lord,　　　　Antistrophe 4 (394–399)
break their skulls with heavy fist?
I'd have the nation's faith restored
and these injustices desist!
Hear, Earth and honored gods below!

CHORUS:

It's surely the law that the spilling of blood　　　Anapests (400–404)
requires additional blood to be spilled.
Violent destruction cries out to a Fury.
She comes from the side of the victims to add
more ruin to previous ruin.

ORESTES:

Popoi-da! Kings of those below,　　　　Strophe 6 (405–409)
potent dead men's Curses, see!
The house of Atreus stands so:
helpless, homeless, her and me.
Zeus, pray tell us where to go,
having lost our family.

CHORUS:

To hear him mourning jolts my heart.   Antistrophe 5 (410–417)
My spirit's dark. I'm in despair.
Then valor comes, distress departs,
and suddenly a light is there.[12]

ELECTRA:

What's the perfect thing to say?   Antistrophe 6 (418–422)
Speak of all that we endure
at Mother's hands to our dismay?
Though she's a skillful flatterer,
her acts cannot be charmed away.
Our wolfish tempers come from her.

CHORUS:

I struck myself as though a Persian born   Strophe 7 (423–428)
and wailed the way barbaric women mourn.
The beating was incessant. One could see
my outstretched hand attacking constantly.
My battered head was full of echoes of
the blows I struck from high, from high above.

ELECTRA:

Ah! Hateful Mother, overbold—   Strophe 8 (429–433)
     his funeral was bare.
He was a royal king, and yet
     no citizens were there.
What arrogance! For even as
     your husband was interred,

---

12. The end of this antistrophe is actually unintelligible as transmitted, and at least one word is missing: "But when once more a strong spirit displaced grief . . . toward a fair prospect for me."

you let no tears be shed for him,
and no lament was heard.

ORESTES:
My father shamed in every way!   Strophe 9 (434–438)
Oh, she will have a price to pay.
The gods and my two hands will see to that.
And once I've bidden her goodbye
forever, I'll be glad to die.

CHORUS:
His corpse was maimed, and you should   Antistrophe 9 (439–443)
    know
that she's the one who did that so
his death would be unbearable for you.
And now you've learned of all the sore
indignities your father bore.

ELECTRA:
You speak of Father's rites. I had no share   Antistrophe 7 (444–450)
of family honors then. I wasn't there,
but scorned as worthless, locked away as though
a rabid dog, I let my teardrops flow.
I'd more of them than laughs. I wept apart.
Inscribe these words of mine upon your heart.

CHORUS:
Do so! Permit her words to pierce   Antistrophe 8 (451–455)
    your ears and calmly tread
upon your heart. Those things were done
    exactly as she said.
The king is watching eagerly.
    He'll have no peace until

he sees the end. You'd better bring
  a strong, unbending will.

ORESTES:
Father, come and help your friends!   Strophe 10 (456–460)

ELECTRA:
Add to his my tearful plea!

CHORUS:
Theirs are prayers this group commends.
Hear! Arise triumphantly!
Destroy our enemies!

ORESTES:
Force fights with force and right with right. Antistrophe 10 (461–465)

ELECTRA:
O gods, dispose these matters well!

CHORUS:
Ah, the fears such prayers excite!
Fate takes its time, and time will tell.
It might respond to prayers.

Eeoo! for troubles families have   Strophe 11 (466–470)
and Ruin's raucous, bloody blow.
For mournful cares that can't be borne
and pains that can't be stopped, eeoo!

Now you yourselves must search your house Antistrophe 11 (471–475)
for lint to stanch the bloody flow,
enduring cruel and deadly strife.
So sing the gods who dwell below.

Blessed divinities under the earth,   Anapests (476–478)
give heed to this prayer and your gracious consent
by sending the children assistance for victory's sake.

ORESTES:
Father, who died deprived of royal rites,   479
I ask that I inherit your estate.   480

ELECTRA:
And Father, I've some things to ask as well:
marriage for me, and for Aegisthus death.[13]

ORESTES:
That way you'll be acclaimed at lawful feasts;
if not, you'll be despised in banquet halls
where people offer savory gifts to Earth.

ELECTRA:
And I'll devote my dowry, all of it,
to pour libations come my wedding day
to honor this, your grave, before all else.

ORESTES:
Earth! send my father up to watch the fight!

ELECTRA:
Persephone, restore his comely strength!   490

ORESTES:
Father, recall the bath that murdered you!

13. Line 482 is unintelligible as transmitted. My reconstruction is based
on the discussion in A. F. Garvie, *Aeschylus: "Choephori,"* 176.

ELECTRA:
Recall the hunter's net that they devised!

ORESTES:
How you were trapped in fetters not of bronze!

ELECTRA:
Disgracefully indeed in scheming sheets!

ORESTES:
Won't such indignities awaken you?

ELECTRA:
Won't you awake and lift your cherished head?

ORESTES:
Send Justice forth to help, or else let us
secure the wrestling grip they used on you,
if you intend to win the second match.

ELECTRA:
And, Father, hear my final desperate prayer!   500
Behold! your nestlings importune your grave.
Pity us both, the male and female line!

ORESTES:
Do not exterminate Pelops's seed!
Although you've died, cheat death by saving me!
[For children are a man's immortal fame.
Like corks they keep the fishing net afloat
and save the lines from sinking out of sight.]¹⁴

14. Lines 505–507 are deleted as an interpolation by most editors.

ELECTRA:
Hear how we're weeping, all for you. Your own
salvation lies in honoring our pleas.

CORYPHAEUS:
I do not fault your lamentation's length,   510
the proper price for mourning long deferred,
but since your mind's determined now to act,
go forth and learn what Fortune has in store!

ORESTES:
I will, but it's in order first to ask
about the queen's belated gifts. Are they
to compensate his fatal suffering?
What feeble courtesy in such a case!
I can't invent the proper simile.
Her gifts are so much smaller than her crime.
In vain you'd empty every jar you own   520
to pay for one man's blood, so people say.
So tell me what her motive was, if known.

CORYPHAEUS:
I know, my child, for I was present then.
The godless woman sent these offerings
in fear of dreams that startled her last night.

ORESTES:
Of dreams? Concerning what? Or can you say?

CORYPHAEUS:
She seemed to bear a serpent, so she said.

ORESTES:
A serpent! Such a dream's significant.

CORYPHAEUS:
She swaddled it as if it were a child.

ORESTES:
What did the infant reptile do for food?　　　　　　530

CORYPHAEUS:
She offered up her breast for it to suck.

ORESTES:
The loathsome creature must have hurt her teat.

CORYPHAEUS:
The milk he sucked included clots of blood.

ORESTES:
How did the woman's vision finally end?

CORYPHAEUS:
She woke completely terrified and screamed.
Then lanterns sunk in darkness came to life,
since everyone was anxious for the queen.
Later she sent these presents here. She hoped
that somehow they'd eliminate her fear.

ORESTES:
I pray to Earth below and Father's tomb　　　　　　540
that this dream vision come to life in me.
I clearly fit the image rather well.
For if the same location first revealed
the snake and me, and it was swaddled too
and sucked the very breasts that nourished me,
mixing the kindly milk with clots of blood,
and she let out an awful scream at that,

it follows that she's doomed to die because
she nursed the dreadful beast, and I'm the snake
who'll be her killer. So the dream declares.   550

CORYPHAEUS:
I like your view of that prophetic dream.
So be it. Still, your allies need advice.
Tell some to act. Have others standing by.

ORESTES:
The plan is simple. She's to go inside

(Indicating ELECTRA.)

and there maintain the strictest secrecy,
so those who killed an honored man by stealth
will fall by stealth themselves and dying feel
the noose that they employed. Apollo says
it shall be so, and he has never lied.
So I'll arrive as though a foreign guest,   560
baggage and all, outside the courtyard gates
with this man, Pylades, a family friend
and ally. We'll affect the speech of Mount
Parnassus, imitating Phocian men.
Suppose a sullen doorman turns us back—
it's possible since evil dwells within.
We'll wait outside so people passing by
the palace gossip, asking questions like:
"Why does Aegisthus bar a suppliant,
if he's at home and knows the fellow's there?"   570
If I get through the courtyard gates and find
Aegisthus sitting on my father's throne,
or he arrives and tries engaging me
in talk, know this. The moment I catch sight

of him, before he asks my native land,
I'll swing my flashing bronze and make a corpse.
Our family's bloated Fury will consume
a third libation, blood and blood alone.

(Addressing ELECTRA.)

Now you attend to household matters well,
lest all these plans we're making come unglued.   580

(Addressing the CHORUS.)

You others, please, when it's appropriate,
be silent. Otherwise, speak cautiously.

(Indicating the statue of Hermes by the palace entrance.)

As for the rest, I ask that Hermes watch
my struggles here and guide my sword aright.

(ELECTRA exits into the palace. ORESTES and PYLADES
return to the parodos.)

CHORUS:
The earth sustains a multitude   Strophe 1 (585–592)
of horrid beasts. Likewise the sea
conceals its own alarming brood,
and often injury

is caused by fire from the sky.
It strikes whatever's in its path,
winged or hoofed, and all decry
a windstorm's violent wrath.

But who could give the measure of Antistrophe 1 (593–601)
men's supreme audacity
or say how wild the shameless love
bold women feel can be?

It's ruinous. Allied with hate,
empowering the female mind,
it undermines the wedded state,
as beast and human find.

Let every man with thoughts well-grounded   Strophe 2 (602–612)
        know
the truth of this, which many stories show.

Think what the bold Althea, Thestiad,
inflammatory female, planned and did![15]

She burned the log, coeval with her son,
age-mate from day of birth till life was done;

for once he gave her womb a parting scream,
his days were numbered by that flaming beam.

15. Althea (al-thē´-ə), daughter of Thestius (thes´-tē-əs; adj. thes´-tē-id), was the mother of the hero Meleager. On the day of his birth, the Fates told her that her infant son would die when a certain log was completely burnt. She retrieved the log from the fire, extinguished the flame, and kept it safe for years. Meleager's claim to fame was that he killed the great wild boar of Calydon. In the wake of that event, he quarreled with his uncles, Althea's brothers, over the disposition of the spoils and ended up killing them. Outraged, Althea threw the magic log into the fire. Meleager died, and Althea killed herself. An early account of Meleager's death appears in an ode by Bacchylides (5.93–155).

Libation Bearers | 113

There is indeed another female who Antistrophe 2 (613–622)
was fit to hate, if what they say is true.

Thanks to a golden necklace she betrayed
her dear old man to death. The bloody maid![16]

For gifts that Minos gave, that bitch would dare
steal her father's death-preventing hair.

She did it while he slept, all safe and sound.
Next thing he knew, lord Hermes came around.[17]

In evil stories, Lemnos[18] *reigns supreme.*[19] Strophe 3 (631–638)
Its infamy is everybody's theme,

and "Lemnian" means anything that's feared.
Thanks to its sin, the race has disappeared,

16. Nisus, the legendary king of Megara, was born with a lock of purple hair and could not be killed as long as he retained it. In time the mighty King Minos (mī´-nəs) of Crete laid siege to Megara. Unable to defeat Nisus by conventional means, he won over Nisus' daughter Scylla with a golden necklace. She cut off her father's hair, he was killed, and Megara fell. Aeschylus' elliptical version is the earliest source for this legend. Ovid, in *Metamorphoses* 8.1–131, gives the earliest full account, in which Scylla betrayed her father because she had fallen in love with Minos.

17. Hermes guides the souls of the dead to the underworld.

18. Another instance of feminine evil. The women of Lemnos were said to have slain all the men of the island for consorting with Thracian concubines. The first detailed account is in Apollonius of Rhodes (1.609–626), but allusions in earlier authors, including Homer (*Iliad* 7.467–471), suggest that the story was well known at an early stage.

19. Here I follow Sommerstein, who reverses the order of 623–630 and 631–638 so that Clytaemestra culminates the chorus's list of dangerous women.

for men dishonor what the gods despise.
Could all these stories be just baseless lies?

Regarding actions famously unkind,　　　　Antistrophe 3 (623–630)
a household-blighting marriage comes to mind,

together with a crafty female plan
against an august military man.[20]

As fires in a hearth must be controlled,
beware a female temper growing bold!

When Justice lies abused,　　　　　　　　Strophe 4 (639–645)
kicked around in mud,
a piercing blade must spill
pulmonary blood,
for someone's violated
custom's strict decree
and shown their disrespect
for Zeus's majesty.

Here Justice stands secure.　　　　　　Antistrophe 4 (646–652)
Her sword is honed by Fate.
A brooding Fury brings
a child to his estate,
polluted by the stains
of blood that linger yet.
He'll wipe the stains away,
and pay the ancient debt.

(ORESTES and PYLADES reenter via a parodos and
approach the palace door.)

20. The chorus is alluding to the murder of Agamemnon.

ORESTES (pounding on the door as he speaks):
Hey, boy! I'm knocking at your courtyard door!   653

>   (ORESTES pauses for a moment, then resumes
>   pounding.)

Hello! Who's there? Is anybody home?

>   (ORESTES again pauses and resumes.)

Here goes my third attempt to summon help,
in hopes Aegisthus welcomes foreign guests.

>   (He pauses and resumes pounding until the DOORMAN
>   speaks.)

DOORMAN (from inside, over ORESTES' pounding):
I hear you, stranger! Tell me where you're from.

ORESTES:
Just call the house's masters. They're the ones
I've come to see. I'm bringing news to them.
The dusky chariot of night draws near.   660
We travelers need to find an anchorage
that harbors every guest. So hurry up!
I want to see the person who's in charge,
the lady running things, or better yet,
her man—for in discussion modesty
obscures your meaning. Men are less
reserved with other men. Then meaning's clear.

>   (The palace doors open, and CLYTAEMESTRA steps
>   outside with her ATTENDANT.)

CLYTAEMESTRA:
What do you strangers need? For everything
that prosperous houses ought to have, we do:
hot baths, a bed to sooth your weary limbs,   670
the company of honest gentlemen.
But if you're seeking something else that takes
official action, I'll inform the men.

ORESTES:
I've come from Phocis.[21] I'm a Daulian.[22]
En route to Argos here, where I can rest
my feet at last—I carried all my things
myself!—an unknown man accosted me.
He claimed to be a Phocian, "Strophius."
We talked about our journeys. Then he said:
"Since you're en route to Argos anyway,   680
please let Orestes' parents know he's dead.
They really must be told, so don't forget.
And bring instructions back when you return.
Either they'll want his ashes carried home
or buried there, exiled eternally.
An urn preserves his ashes now inside
its metal walls. His death was duly mourned."
That's all the stranger said. Do I by chance
address Orestes' legal guardian
or relative? His father needs to know.   690

CLYTAEMESTRA:
I'm devastated, crushed, and overthrown!

21. Phocis (fō´-kəs), a district in central Greece where the oracle of
Delphi was located.
22. Daulia (dȯ´-lē-ə; adj. dȯ´-lē-ən), a town in Phocis close to Delphi.

Old family curse, malicious wrestler!
You see so clearly, even distant things.
The arrows you release from far away
with pinpoint aim are stripping me of friends.
And now you've killed Orestes—even though
he'd sense enough to skirt this deadly swamp.
We'd hoped he'd be our frenzy's antidote.
Well, call that hope just one more traitor now.

ORESTES:
I only wish that I had better news   700
by way of introduction, seeing my hosts
so clearly blest as you. Does any bond
surpass the one uniting guest and host?
Yet I felt duty-bound to undertake
this heavy task. I told my friends I would,
and I was welcomed graciously by you.

CLYTAEMESTRA:
You'll be rewarded no less worthily
for that, nor be considered less a friend.
We would have heard the news from someone else.
But now's the time for daylong travelers   710
to have the comforts lengthy journeys earn.

(Addressing her ATTENDANT.)

Show him and his companion here the way
to where the men's apartments are. Make sure
that their reception dignifies our house.
I'm holding you responsible for that.

(Turning back to ORESTES and PYLADES.)

Meanwhile, I'll see the master hears your news,
and since we haven't quite run out of friends,
we'll also be discussing it with them.

(All exit into the palace.)

CORYPHAEUS:
Dear women who serve in this house,   Anapests (719–729)
say when will we finally employ
the power of speech on behalf of Orestes.

CHORUS (praying):
Your majesties, Earth and the mound
that covers the naval commander's
royal remains, be attentive
and come to our aid, for it's time
for deceptive Persuasion to enter
the fray and for underworld Hermes,
the lord of the night, to observe
these men in the deadly ordeal of the sword.

(CILISSA enters from the palace.)

CORYPHAEUS:
I think our guest is causing trouble now.   730
I see Orestes' nursemaid full of tears.

(Addressing CILISSA.)

What brings you here, Cilissa, past the gates,
unhired grief your only company?[23]

23. Cilissa is not a paid mourner. Her grief is genuine.

CILISSA:

The queen instructed me to go and bring
Aegisthus back to see our visitors,
so he can hear their story man-to-man
in greater depth. Since there were servants there,
she tried to look distressed but barely hid
her inward joy at recent happenings—
so good for her, so evil otherwise.   740
I mean the strangers' shocking news. And now,
Aegisthus! He'll be overjoyed to hear
the story. What intolerable pain!
The ancient stew of grief inside this house
of Atreus is truly hard to bear.
It breaks my heart! But I have never yet
endured a sorrow comparable to this.
I soldiered on through all the other ones,
but dear Orestes gone! I gave my life
to him. I suckled him when newly born.   750
His shrill demands at night prevented sleep.
Nothing I tried accomplished anything.
A child's irrational, an animal.
Its nurse's guesses are the only guide.
A babe in diapers can't express a thing:
its hunger, thirst, its need to urinate.
The immature intestine has no rules.
I tried to prophesy but often failed,
and had to be a washerwoman then,
an infant's nurse and laundry maid in one.   760
Because I had that pair of homely skills,
the king entrusted him to me to raise.
So hearing that he's dead was terrible.
And now I'm off to see this house's bane,
and he'll be very glad to hear the news.

CORYPHAEUS:
How did she order him to come equipped?

CILISSA:
How what? Ask that again—more clearly,
        though.

CORYPHAEUS:
Was he to come with soldiers or alone?

CILISSA:
She said to bring attendants armed with spears.

CORYPHAEUS:
Don't tell our hated master that, but say   770
to come alone "to ease the strangers' fears."
Do that as quickly as you can, and smile!
Good messengers assist a limping tale.

CILISSA:
You seem so happy. Why? The recent news?

CORYPHAEUS:
Zeus can reverse an evil wind, you know.

CILISSA:
But how? Our only hope, Orestes, died.

CORYPHAEUS:
Not yet. A bad diviner told you that.

CILISSA:
Say what? Have you got knowledge others don't?

CORYPHAEUS:
Go! Follow orders! Be our messenger.
The gods watch over things they care about.   780

CILISSA:
All right, I'll go and follow your advice,
hope for the best and gods' assistance too.

(Exit CILISSA.)

CHORUS:
Father of the deities   Strophe 1 (783–788)
of Mount Olympus, hear me please!
Let our masters find their way.
They yearn to see the light of day.[24]
There's Justice in my every word.
Zeus, may you preserve it!

Zeus, let the man who's gone within   Mesode (789–792)
confront his enemies and win.
Let his reputation soar.
He'll pay you back two times or more.

The orphaned colt of your dear steed   Antistrophe 1 (793–799)
is yoked to grief. Control his speed.
Establish rhythm in his run
until the race is finally won

24. Lines 785 and 786 are unintelligible as transmitted. The general
sense is a wish that Orestes and Electra succeed. They are said to be yearning
to see something. My conjectural reconstruction of the sense is based on
Garvie, *Choephori*, 257, endorsed in Sommerstein, *Oresteia*, 311, that the word
for light, phōs, was part of the original. For light as a metaphor for peace and
prosperity, compare *Agamemnon* 522.

and we have seen the countryside
pass beneath his feet.

Friendly deities who guard   Strophe 2 (800–806)
   the house's wealth, pay heed!
Wipe blood away with just revenge
   until this family's freed
from stains of ancient slaughter. Let
   old murders cease to breed.

O awesome cavern's lord,[25] *we beg of you,*   Mesode (807–811)
permit his house to raise its head and view
with happy eyes the light of freedom through
its murky veil.

And Maia's child[26] *should also help.*   Antistrophe 2 (812–818)
   He wafts things on their way,
often bringing light to dark,
   but also likes to play
with cryptic words, obscure by night
   and just as dark by day.

At last to help the ship   Strophe 3 (819–825)
that comes to set us free,
we'll cast a magic spell
to calm the winds at sea,
a female song like this:

25. By the process of elimination, the god invoked is probably Apollo, whose role in Orestes' story is so important. He is identified as one inhabiting a great and well-constructed *stomion*, the diminutive of *stoma* (mouth) used to denote cave mouths. The passage may refer to some feature of Apollo's temple at Delphi.

26. Hermes, the child of Maia (mā´-ə), a lesser goddess, and Zeus.

"How well the voyage ends!
The gains belong to me,
and Ruin spares my friends."[27]

Have courage when you start the deed,   Mesode (826–830)
and if she calls you "Child!" exclaim:
"That's right! My father's!" Then proceed.
The act's a sin, but free of blame.

Show Perseus's heart,[28]   Antistrophe 3 (831–837)
to those to whom you're bound,
your ghostly friends below
and those above the ground.
Bring bloody ruin to
the baneful Gorgon here.
Pluck the seed of guilt
and make it disappear.

(Enter AEGISTHUS.)

AEGISTHUS:
I'm here! A messenger invited me.   838
I hear some strangers brought the opposite
of pleasing news: they said Orestes met   840
his fated end. If so, our family has
another blood-soaked burden hard to bear,
while ancient murders sting and fester still.
But is the strangers' story accurate

27. See Garvie, *Choephori*, 268: "Such is the power of the spoken word
that the Chorus think of it as effecting the action which more logically it
merely accompanies. It has a ritual, even a magical, quality."

28. Perseus is the mythical hero who slew the Gorgon Medusa with help
from Hermes.

or merely women's talk, just words that fly
around, then finally fall to earth and die?
Can you enlighten me in that regard?

CORYPHAEUS:
Although we heard the story, you should go
inside and ask the strangers. Second-hand
reports can't vie with talking man-to-man.   850

AEGISTHUS:
You're right. I'd better see the man and learn
if he was there the day Orestes died
or just repeats some hazy tale he heard.
He won't deceive my sharp-eyed intellect!

(Exit AEGISTHUS into the palace.)

CHORUS:
O Zeus, tell me what I should say,   Anapests (855–868)
tell me how to begin my appeal,
what are the words I should use
to signal my friendly intentions.
For murderous blades are preparing
their bloody endeavors, and either
the Agamemnonian house
will experience utter destruction,
will perish eternally, or
Orestes will celebrate freedom
with fire and light and inherit
the power to govern the city
and the marvelous wealth of his father.

Divinely inspired, Orestes
girds for a wrestling match,

a contest of two against one.
He sat through the previous round,
and now he will fight by himself.
May victory cap his attempt!

AEGISTHUS (within):
Eee! Eee! Otótotoí!   869

CORYPHAEUS:
Oh, oh!   870
What's the noise from the house? What's occurred?
Let's give this troubled place a wider berth.
We need to look completely uninvolved.
The battle's done. It's been decided now.

            (A SERVANT enters from the palace.)

SERVANT:
Oimoi! Oimoi! They've struck the master down!
Oimoi! again, a triple cry of grief!
Aegisthus isn't . . . any longer. Open up!
Come on! Be quick! Unbar the women's gates.[29]
We'll also need a muscular young man,
but not to help the murdered one, of course.   880
Hello! Hello!
I'm wasting breath! They're deaf or sound asleep.
And where has Clytaemestra gone? And why?

29. The frantic servant's reference to the women's gates raises the
possibility that the skēnē's exterior had a second entrance reserved for
women. It is equally possible and simpler to imagine that the women's
quarters, with their locked entrance, were imagined to be inside the skēnē
and that the servant stood outside the main entrance shouting toward
them.

The chances are her head's about to fall
beside a chopping block when Justice strikes.

(CLYTAEMESTRA enters from the women's quarters.)

CLYTAEMESTRA:
What *is* it? What's this shouting all about?

SERVANT:
Dead men are murdering the living now.[30]

CLYTAEMESTRA:
Ah, so! I understand your riddling words.
We'll die the way we killed, by clever tricks.
Bring me a lethal weapon! Get an ax!
We'll either win or lose. So let's find out!   890
I've finally reached the peak of misery.

(Exit SERVANT frantically through the main doors. He
passes ORESTES on the way out.)

ORESTES:
It's you I'm looking for. I'm done with him.

(Indicating the interior of the palace where he has killed
AEGISTHUS.)

30. In the Greek, "the dead" is plural but "the living" is singular. The
servant's meaning seems to be that the reputedly dead Orestes and Agamemnon's ghost are in the process of killing the living Aegisthus, but his words are
ambiguous. They could be interpreted as a generalized observation: ghosts
are killing living people these days. The Greek would even allow the subject
and object to be interchanged: a living man, Orestes, is killing people who
are as good as dead—first Aegisthus and next Clytaemestra.

CLYTAEMESTRA:
My dear Aegisthus, are you truly dead?

(PYLADES[31] appears in the main doorway. Perhaps he
has dispatched the SERVANT who was looking for an ax
for CLYTAEMESTRA.)

ORESTES:
Since he's your lover, share a tomb with him.
That way you won't betray his lifeless corpse.

CLYTAEMESTRA (baring a breast):
No, wait, my child, my son, and pity this,
the breast you sucked with infant gums while half
asleep and drank the milk that nourished you.

ORESTES:
Well, should I spare her? Answer, Pylades!

PYLADES (emerging from the doorway):
Then what about Apollo's oracles   900
and binding vows exchanged at Pytho's shrine?
Offend all men before you anger gods.

ORESTES:
You win the contest, friend. That's good advice.

31. Tragedians competing at the festival of Dionysus were limited in the
number of speaking actors they could employ for financial reasons: the state
paid the actors' salaries. In composing the *Oresteia*, Aeschylus was limited to
three actors. Hence, since actors one and two were needed to play Orestes
and Clytaemestra, the third actor had to exit as the terrified servant and return as Pylades in order to speak his only lines in the play. He had less than a
minute to change masks and personalities.

(To CLYTAEMESTRA, while motioning toward the palace doors.)

You, follow me. I'll kill you next to him,
a better man than father while alive,
or so you thought. You'll join your lover there
in death, while hating one you should have loved.

CLYTAEMESTRA:
I nursed you once. Let's age together too!

ORESTES:
My father's killer wants to live with me!

CLYTAEMESTRA:
Fate played a role in all those matters, child.   910

ORESTES:
And Fate has got another death in store.

CLYTAEMESTRA:
But don't you fear a mother's curse, my child?

ORESTES:
You bore me, then abandoned me to grief.

CLYTAEMESTRA:
That *was* an ally's home I sent you to!

ORESTES:
You sold me cheaply, me a noble's son!

CLYTAEMESTRA:
Then where's the profit I received for you?

ORESTES:
The answer would humiliate us both.

CLYTAEMESTRA:
But weren't your father's follies just as bad?

ORESTES:
He labored mightily while you relaxed.

CLYTAEMESTRA:
It's hard for women—being without a man.   920

ORESTES:
Men work to feed their idle wives at home.

CLYTAEMESTRA:
You seem resolved to kill your mother, son.

ORESTES:
I'm not to blame. The killer's really you.

CLYTAEMESTRA:
Take care! Beware your mother's dogged curse.

ORESTES:
I can't escape my father's otherwise.

CLYTAEMESTRA:
I might as well be talking to a tomb!

ORESTES:
Yes. Father's blood decided everything.

CLYTAEMESTRA:
You! You're the deadly snake I bore and fed!

ORESTES:
Your dreams awoke prophetic fears. But now,
for lawless murder, undergo the same!   930

> (CLYTAEMESTRA, ORESTES, and PYLADES exit
> through the main doors.)

CORYPHAEUS:
I feel some pity seeing that couple fall,
but since the bold Orestes is the one
who's gained the peak of bloodshed, I approve.
His family's light will not become extinct.

CHORUS:
As Justice reached the Priamids in time,   Strophe 1 (935–941)
with heavy-handed punishment for crime,
so lion twins, twin votaries of war,
have broken through King Agamemnon's door.
His thoughts inflamed by god, the exiled man
has crossed the finish line of Delphi's plan.

Raise up a cheer! The master's house is free   Mesode (942–945)
from evil days and waste of property
by that malignant pair. Oh horrid fate!

The crafty goddess Recompense was there—   Antistrophe 1 (946–952)
deceptive strategy her special care,[32]
but Zeus's daughter steered Orestes' hand
throughout the battle. Men who understand
her nature call her Justice, one who breathes
destructive wrath against her enemies!

32. Recompense or Penalty personified (*poinē* in Greek) sees to it
that people always pay for their sins, often by an indirect and unexpected
route.

Loxias, who rules　　　　　　　　　　Strophe 2 (953–960)
the Delphic gorge, proclaimed
without deceit she'd been
deceitfully defamed.
But she's attacking now.
Her time has finally come.
God finds a remedy
for every evil done.
Heaven's government
must be revered.

Now we can see the light. You've loosed　　　　Mesode (961–964)
　　your house's giant chain.
Dear house, arise at last—depart
　　the mud in which you've lain.

Soon our sovereign chief　　　　　Antistrophe 2 (965–971)
will make his way outside,
once the house's hearth
is thoroughly purified
by rites of expiation,
purging deadly crimes.
He'll bring the fortunes back
we saw in former times,
with wholly friendly smiles
like gracious guests.[33]

(The palace doors open, revealing ORESTES standing over the bodies of CLYTAEMESTRA and AEGISTHUS. ORESTES holds a bloody sword in one hand; an olive wreath in the other hand symbolizes his status as a suppliant.)

33. Line 972, a repetition of line 961, is deleted by Sommerstein and others.

ORESTES:
Behold! The nation's double tyranny,   973
my father's house-despoiling murderers!
They were a stately pair on thrones before,
and they're a loving couple still, to judge
by looks. They've also kept their promises.
They swore they'd see my wretched father dead,
then welcome death themselves,[34] and so they have.

(Several SERVANTS enter from the palace carrying
what looks like a rolled-up rug.)

My listeners, there's evil yet to tell.   980
See what they trapped my wretched father with,
the thing that bound his hands and shackled feet.   982
Now this contrivance—what's the proper name?[35]   997
A way to catch a hunted beast? A shroud?   998
A robe for bathing? No! The proper term's   999
a snare, a net, a foot-entangling gown.   1000
A man who made a living swindling   1001
his guests, relieving them of silver coins,   1002
could use this cunning trap. He could amuse   1003

---

34. A reference to the cliché that one can die happy (or is happy to die)
once some longed-for event has occurred; compare *Agamemnon* 539, 1610–
1611; *Libation Bearers* 438.

35. Orestes' speech from 973 to 1006 is somewhat incoherent. (Some
critics suggest that his madness has already set in!) Specifically, lines 997–
1004 seem clearly out of place. The preceding lines, 991–996, are a denuncia-
tion of Clytaemestra. Instead of rounding that off with the statement that he
would never choose to live with such a woman (1005–1006), he reverts to a
horrified description of the robe she used in killing Agamemnon (997–1004).
Order seems to be restored by the suggestion in Garvie, *Choephori*, 326–27,
of putting lines 997–1004 after line 982.

himself by killing everyone he met.	1004
You servants, coming close, unfold the thing	983
and show the people what a dread device[36]	983a
it is for trapping victims hopelessly.	984

(The SERVANTS, stepping forward, unfold the robe, a huge woolen garment. It was once brightly embroidered. Those colors have faded, but not the bright red bloodstains.)

Let Father see—not mine,

(Indicating AGAMEMNON's tomb.)

but father Sun,	985
who sees all earthly things. Let him observe	
my mother's impure handiwork. Some day	
he might bear witness, say her death was just.	
I won't discuss Aegisthus. He's just paid	
the customary price for lechery.	990
But she who made this loathsome thing to kill	
the man whose babes her womb protected once—	
her loving children, now her bitter foes—	
what's she? A snake? A moray eel perhaps?	
Why not? Her very touch was poisonous,	
so evil was her daring, twisted mind.	996
May no such woman ever live with me!	1005
O gods, I'd rather die without an heir.	1006

36. The scholia to Euripides' *Orestes* 25 attribute to Aeschylus a line saying, "a device that could not be resisted or stripped off." M. L. West, in *Studies in Aeschylus*, 262, suggests that it belongs in this passage. The suggestion is adopted by Sommerstein, *Oresteia*, 338. My translation incorporates its sense in lines 983a–984.

CHORUS:

What pitiful, pitiful deeds! Strophe 1 (1007–1009)
You perished in horrible pain,
and flowers of further distress
are blooming for those who remain.

ORESTES:

Is she the guilty one or not? This robe 1010
shows how she wet the sword Aegisthus brought,
this robe that gleamed with many colors once,
though it's disfigured now by time and blood.
Now I can praise the man in person, weep
and moan, denounce the robe that murdered him.
And yet, I pity all of us—our deeds,
our suffering, my tainted victory.

CHORUS:

No mortal lives a life Antistrophe 1 (1018–1020)
completely trouble-free.
Some trials the future brings,
and some come instantly.

ORESTES:

So that you know, I cannot tell you how 1021
this thing will end. My rebel mind is like
a chariot careening uncontrolled.
I'm carried off, and Panic waits beside
my heart to sing and dance to Hatred's tune.
But while I'm lucid, I declare to friends:
my mother's death was justified. In her,
I killed my father's bloodstained murderer,
loathed by the gods. The potion making me
so bold was Pytho's prophet, Loxias. 1030
If I succeeded, I'd be free of blame,

he said. If not, I'd suffer horribly.
No archer's shaft could reach that height of pain.
Take note of all my preparations now.
Wearing this wreath of olives, I'll approach
Apollo's sacred ground, the navel stone[37]
and its renowned immortal flame; and there
I'll fight the charge of spilling kindred blood.
Apollo steered me toward that hearth alone.
I say to all the Argives: (keep) this tale   1040
of evils (fresh in memory) and testify   1041a
for me (if) Menelaus (does return).[38]   1041b
Now I'll become a banished vagabond,   1042
in life and death, my reputation this: 1043a
(a loving son, I took my mother's life).[39]   1043b

CORYPHAEUS:
You acted well! Don't stain your mouth with foul
rebukes. Don't utter such ill-omened words.
You freed the Argive state by cutting off
two serpent heads with great dexterity.

ORESTES:
Ah!
What sort of Gorgon women now appear

37. A boulder kept at Delphi and viewed as a sacred object. It was said to mark the center of the earth. At the beginning of *Eumenides* Orestes is discovered clinging to it for protection from the Furies.

38. Line 1041 as transmitted ("and bear witness for me, Menelaus, how evil things happened") is apparently a garbled combination of two lines conflated by scribal error. My translation follows the rearrangement of the extant words with some conjectural restorations in Sommerstein, *Oresteia*, 344.

39. Line 1043b is a conjectural restoration of a line that has apparently dropped out of the manuscript. Without it, Orestes' speech concludes with an unexplained reference to "this" (i.e., the following) reputation.

in pitch-black robes and wreaths of writhing snakes?
So many writhing snakes! I can't stay here.   1050

CORYPHAEUS:
What visions madden you? Stand still! Fear not!
You've won and earned your father's fondest love.

ORESTES:
These aren't mere visions tracking me. Oh no,
I see them clearly: Mother's rabid hounds!

CORYPHAEUS:
Maternal blood still moistening your hands—
that's surely why you're feeling so distraught.

ORESTES:
O lord Apollo, how they multiply!
Their eyes are dripping ghastly tears of blood.

CORYPHAEUS:
Apollo's touch alone will set you free
from suffering. The god's your only hope.   1060

ORESTES:
You cannot see the monsters hunting me.
I do. They're getting close. I can't stay here.

        (Exit ORESTES terrified.)

CORYPHAEUS:
Farewell! Some kindly god watch over you,
with helpful bits of luck along the way!

        (While chanting, the CHORUS marches back into
        palace.)

CHORUS:

Three tempests have shaken this house,
precipitous, perilous storms.
They howled and subsided. The first
was the horrible slaughter of children.
A monarch's ordeal happened next.
The Achaeans' commander and chief
was murdered while taking a bath.
And now, out of somewhere, a third
salvation, or should I say "doom"?
Oh, where is the end, the completion,
the day when the power of Ruin
will finally be lulled back to sleep?

Anapests (1065–1076)

The Holy Goddesses;
formerly, Eumenides

Characters

PYTHIA, the priestess of Apollo at Delphi
ORESTES, Agamemnon's son
APOLLO, god of prophecy, also called Phoebus and Loxias
HERMES, divine herald and messenger of the gods
GHOST OF CLYTAEMESTRA, Orestes' mother
CHORUS, Furies
CORYPHAEUS, the leader of the chorus
ATHENA, goddess of Athens, also called Pallas
HERALD
JURORS, eleven Athenian citizens
SECOND CHORUS, Athena's attendants

> (The play opens outside APOLLO's temple at Delphi.
> His priestess, the PYTHIA, stands in front of the doors
> to pray before entering the temple.)

PYTHIA:
The god my prayers will honor first is Earth,
the first true prophet; Themis[1] after her,
the second deity to occupy

---

1. Themis (thē'-mis), a goddess personifying traditional law.

the gods' prophetic throne, or so we're told.[2]
The third, the Titan Phoebe, born of Earth,
took over next by Themis's consent,
not force, and yields her place to Phoebus now,
a birthday gift for one who bears her name.[3]
He left the lake on rocky Delos then,
docked at Athena's ship-frequented shore,   10
and entered this Parnassian abode.
Sons of Hephaestus[4] built a thoroughfare,
escorting him with utmost reverence;
they smoothed the rugged ground along the way.
Once he arrived, the people worshipped him.

2. Aeschylus' history of Delphi looks like an invention based on Hesiod's
Theogony. There Earth (Gaia) is the first deity to emerge from Chaos (116–
118). She produces Heaven (Uranus) to be her husband (126–127). The twelve
Titans, including Themis and Phoebe, result from their union (133–137).
Themis' claim to fame is that she is the mother of the three Fates by Zeus
(901–906). Phoebe is the mother of Leto and Hecate by a male Titan, Coeus
(404–412). Leto is one of Zeus's many brides and the mother by him of Apollo
and Artemis (918–920). Aeschylus represents the history of Delphi as a series
of gifts, beginning when Mother Earth voluntarily passes control of the shrine
to her daughter Themis. In contrast, the traditional version of the myth has
Apollo taking over Delphi by force when he slays a great serpent symbolic of
Earth's power and taunts the dying beast by telling him to "rot" (*pythe!* in
Greek). Hence Delphi was also known as Pytho and its chief priestess as the
Pythia (*Homeric Hymn to Apollo* 355–374).

3. Phoebus (fē´-bəs), an adjective meaning "bright" or "radiant" in
Greek. Phoebe (fē´-bē), the goddess's name, is the feminine form of the
adjective. Apollo assumed its masculine form as a surname to honor his
grandmother.

4. Erichthonius, first Athenian king by some accounts, was born from
earth impregnated by Hephaestus' semen, which he spilled in a clumsy attempt
to rape Athena. See Apollodorus' *Library* 3.187–190 for details.

Their lord and steersman Delphus[5] did so too.
Zeus gave Apollo's mind inspired skill
and made him fourth of prophets seated here.
He's Zeus's spokesman known as Loxias.
So much for my preliminary prayers.   20
I honor Pallas first among the rest.
Corycian nymphs[6] receive my worship too
inside their haunted, bird-infested cave.
And I remember Bromios, who rules
the land, became the Bacchants' general
and god, and snared the rabbit Pentheus.[7]
At last with nods to Pleistos,[8] mountain stream,
Poseidon's[9] might, and Zeus on high who brings
all things to pass, I take my mantic seat.
Of all my visits, gods, make this the best.   30

If any Greeks stand by, draw lots and come
accordingly, for that's the practice here.
I prophesy however god commands.[10]

---

5. Delphus (del´-fəs) is probably an Aeschylean invention inspired by
the place name "Delphi."

6. The Corycian (cə-ri´-shən) Cave is a large cavern in Parnassus, not
far from Delphi. The name seems derived from *korykos* (a leather sack). The
Corycian nymphs were its resident deities. Archaeologists have recovered a
huge number of votive offerings from the cave.

7. Bromios (brō´-mē-əs), "the boisterous one," is another name for Dionysus, god of wine. When his worship was scorned in Thebes by the regent
Pentheus (pen´thē-əs), Dionysus drove his women followers, the Bacchants
(ba´-känts), to kill him. Euripides' *Bacchae* tells the story.

8. Pleistos (plī´-stəs), a stream that flows down Mount Parnassus near
Delphi.

9. Poseidon (pō-sī´-dən), the great god of the sea.

10. Delphi was an oracular temple. In its central ceremony, Apollo took

The Holy Goddesses

(PYTHIA exits into the temple, leaving the stage empty
for several long moments. She finally scurries out,
crawling on hands and knees like a little child.)

Things terrible to see or even name
have chased me out of Loxias's house—
so terrible that I can't even stand.
My hands must do my running, not my legs.
A scared old woman's nothing but a child!
Nearing my inner shrine, where garlands hang,
I saw a man beside the navel stone,[11]   40
a filthy, god-forsaken criminal
turned suppliant. His hands and steaming sword
were dripping blood. He held an olive branch,
immense and tastefully adorned with wreaths
of glistening wool. I don't remember more.
In front of him reclined a shocking troupe
of women, slouching, sound asleep on thrones.
Not women, really. Gorgons possibly—
but even that is not the perfect term.
I've seen a painting where some female things   50
are robbing Phineus's food,[12] but these

---

possession of the Pythia and responded through her to questions posed by
pilgrims who came from all over the Greek world seeking divine advice. Here
the Pythia opens the shrine for business.

11. A boulder kept at Delphi and viewed as a sacred object. It was said to
mark the center of the earth. Orestes clings to it for protection as though a
god's altar.

12. Phineus (fī´-nē-əs) was a prophet blinded by Zeus for revealing too
much and tormented by Harpies, monstrous birdwomen who stole his food,
leaving only an unbearable stench behind. Jason and the Argonauts drove the
Harpies away in return for Phineus' inspired advice. See Apollonius of
Rhodes 1.120–123.

The Holy Goddesses | 143

were wingless, black all over, truly foul.
Their snores and snorts would knock a person down.
Their eyes rained putrid streams across their cheeks.
Their clothing wasn't fit for one to wear
in human homes, much less in holy shrines.
I've never seen the like nor ever heard
a nation boast of raising such a horde
without the effort causing deep regret.
But now it's up to master Loxias   60
himself, the mighty god, to handle them.
Physician, seer, prophet, he's the one
in charge of purging homes for other gods.

(The PYTHIA exits via a parodos. The temple doors
open, revealing the interior. A representation of the
navel stone, a boulder covered by wool, rests in the
middle. ORESTES sits in front of it. He matches the
PYTHIA's description: he holds a bloody sword in one
hand and a long olive branch with a woolen wreath on
top in the other. Barely visible in the interior darkness
are APOLLO and HERMES and a couple of FURIES,
who sleep slouched in chairs. At length, ORESTES rises
to pray.)

ORESTES:
You recognize and shun what isn't just,[13]   85
my lord Apollo. Shun indifference too.   86
Your strength is capable of doing good.   87

13. I follow the suggestion of Oliver Taplin in *The Stagecraft of Aeschylus*,
364, by transposing lines 85–88 from their original location to the beginning
of the episode. This obviates the difficulty of having Apollo start his speech in
mid-thought. Sommerstein, *Oresteia*, transposes only lines 85–87.

APOLLO:

Remember that and don't succumb to fear.   88
Nearby or far, I won't abandon you.   64
I'll be your faithful guard until the end.
Your enemies will never find me kind.
You see these raging female prisoners,
these ancient virgins sunk in slumber now,
these gray and withered maids, with whom no god
nor any man or beast has intercourse.   70
They are innately evil; hence they dwell
beneath the earth in evil Tartarus
despised by mortal men and higher gods.
Therefore I tell you, flee these creatures now!
They'll follow you across the continent
as you traverse the solid land, and then
they'll cross the sea and enter sea-girt towns.
Don't be discouraged pondering this toil.
Until you reach Athena's city, run!
Then sit and hug her ancient image there.   80
Equipped with jurymen and winning words,
we'll find the means of liberating you
from all these tribulations evermore.
I *made* you kill your mother, after all.   84

(Turning to HERMES.)

Brother by blood, your father same as mine,[14]   89
Hermes, protect my servant. Justify   90
your title. Be his guide. Let him return,
escorted well, to mortal company.
Zeus holds such homeless men in high regard.

14. Apollo and Hermes were sons of Zeus by the goddesses Leto and
Maia, respectively.

(APOLLO recedes into the shadows. HERMES takes ORESTES by the hand, and they run out of the temple and exit along a parodos. When they are gone, the GHOST OF CLYTAEMESTRA appears. Perhaps she rises from behind the navel stone, where she has crouched unseen from the outset.)

GHOST OF CLYTAEMESTRA (addressing the sleeping FURIES):
You'd sleep? *O-ay!* What good does sleeping do?
The other corpses have contempt for me
because of you. I'm always being rebuked
among the dead for killing those I did
and wander like a tramp. I tell you this,
the reason I've incurred the greatest blame—
despite my own atrocious suffering—   100
is that no angry god avenges me,
though I was killed by matricidal hands.
Let hearts and eyes behold these bleeding wounds!   103
You've lapped those wineless offerings of mine,[15]   106
libations meant to soothe the sober tongue.
You've shared nocturnal feasts beside my hearth,
at hours when no other gods were there.
But all of that's been trampled underfoot,   110
and he's escaping like a little fawn,
easily jumping over hunting nets
and laughing oh so heartily at you.
I'm begging you to save my very soul!

15. Lines 104 and 105 are probably an interpolation: "The sleeping mind is clear-sighted, / while mortal men are blind to fate by day." As Sommerstein, *Aeschylus: Eumenides*, 103, points out, the two lines seem to belong together, but 105 has no relevance to the situation at hand.

The Holy Goddesses

Oh hear me, buried goddesses, awake!
The ghost of Clytaemestra's calling you!

(The FURIES snore.)

GHOST OF CLYTAEMESTRA:
Stop snoring! Weep! The man's eluded you.

(Sarcastically.)

Some suppliants have helpful friends, it seems.

(The FURIES snore.)   120

GHOST OF CLYTAEMESTRA:
You're sound asleep, ignoring all my pain.
Meanwhile a matricide is going free!

(Various FURIES cry out as if having a bad dream.)

CHORUS:
Oh! Oh!

GHOST OF CLYTAEMESTRA:
You're shouting "oh!" while still asleep? Get up!
You're good for nothing but inflicting pain!

(Other FURIES cry Oh! The GHOST OF CLYTAE-
MESTRA notices that the snakes in the FURIES' hair are
limp and lifeless.)

So—sleep and labor, arch conspirators,
can even drain a deadly serpent's strength!

(The FURIES emit high-pitched moans, as though
beginning to wake up.)

CHORUS:
Oh catch him! Catch him! Hurry! There he goes!   130

GHOST OF CLYTAEMESTRA:
It's not a beast you're chasing—it's a dream—
and yet you're growling like a pack of hounds!
What are you doing? Stand! You can't give up!
Forget your nap! Remember my distress
and feel the bitter sting of just complaints.
Correctly understood, they're merely goads.
A certain back should feel your bloody breath.
Get after him! Go belch the flames in which
he'll melt. A second race will do him in!

(The ghost disappears by sinking back down behind
the navel stone. The CORYPHAEUS and CHORISTERS
rise from their chairs or stream out of the interior darkness across the stage and into the orchēstra. As they do
so, their hideous masks and headdresses full of snakes
become visible for the first time. The CORYPHAEUS
shakes a nearby CHORISTER awake.)

CORYPHAEUS:
Wake that one up, like I've awakened you!   140
Still sleeping? Up! Shake off that drowsy look!
Let's see if she was wasting breath just now.

(As each CHORISTER enters the orchēstra, she sings or
recites a metrical line. Starting with the second strophe,

the CORYPHAEUS and twelve CHORISTERS perform
the rest of the ode in the normal way.)

CHORISTER 1:
Eeoo! Popax! We've suffered, friends!   Strophe 1 (143–148)

CHORISTER 2:
I surely have—and suffered all in vain!

CHORISTER 3:
Popoi! We've suffered terribly!

CHORISTER 4:
Could anybody stand the pain?

CHORISTER 5:
The beast was snared but got away.

CHORISTER 6:
I fell asleep and lost my prey.

CHORISTER 7:
O Zeus's son, you're quite the thief!   Antistrophe 1 (149–154)

CHORISTER 8:
You've trampled underfoot the elder gods.

CHORISTER 9:
A god, you saved a matricide,

CHORISTER 10:
a godless man at bitter odds

CHORISTER 11:
with every parent. Who would say

CHORISTER 12:
that that was just in any way?

CHORUS:
The criticisms that I heard   Strophe 2 (155–161)
in dreams have stung my heart and mind
They struck me like those wagoners
who goad their horses from behind.
I feel the icy pain as though
I'm scourged by one who's none too kind,
some public executioner.

How the younger gods behave!   Antistrophe 2 (162–168)
How absolute their rule has grown!
One can see the blood and gore
enveloping the Delphic throne.
One can sense the curse of blood
that's clinging to the navel stone,
the foul pollution it's incurred.

The seer god—without a reason why—   Strophe 3 (169–172)
let foul pollution stain his inner shrine.
The ancient Fates were left to wilt and die.
He honored human law and broke divine.

He angered me as well, but never fear.   Antistrophe 3 (173–178)
The beggar won't escape although he's fled
beneath the earth. For when he runs from here,
another vengeful judge will have his head.

    (APOLLO steps forward from the shadows and addresses
    the FURIES.)

APOLLO:
I order you to leave my residence   179
at once! Vacate my inner sanctum! Go!   180
If not, you'll feel a flashing viper's bite,
the winged snake my golden bowstring shoots.
You'll retch and vomit up the frothy blood
and clotted gore you've sucked from mortal
        men.
Propriety forbids your presence here.
Depart to where beheadings are, where eyes
are gouged and gullets slit, where little boys
are gelded, others stoned and maimed or moan
and cry for mercy, mercy! dying impaled
on iron spikes. Yes, that's the horrid sort   190
of godless celebration you enjoy.
Abominable! Your every feature says
the same. You're clearly fit to live in caves
with blood-soaked lions—not deposit filth
around this sacred place of oracles.
So leave without a herdsman, vagrant goats!
No god has friendly thoughts for such a flock.

CORYPHAEUS:
My lord, Apollo, hear our words in turn.
You are yourself no mere accomplice here.
From first to last, the guilt's entirely yours.   200

APOLLO:
How so? Say just enough to answer that.

CORYPHAEUS:
You steered your temple's guest toward matricide.

APOLLO:
I said, "Avenge your father's death!" So what?

CORYPHAEUS:
You promised you'd receive him wet with blood.

APOLLO:
I ordered him to supplicate my shrine.

CORYPHAEUS:
But why abuse his escort — namely, us?

APOLLO:
Your presence here is hardly suitable.

CORYPHAEUS:
We can't perform our function otherwise.

APOLLO:
Your function? Really! What, pray tell, is that?

CORYPHAEUS:
We chase all mother-killers far away.   210

APOLLO:
And what about a husband-killing wife?

CORYPHAEUS:
No kindred blood is spilt in such a case.

APOLLO:
You thus disparage pledges made by Zeus
and Hera, who perfects the marriage bond.
Your words dishonor Aphrodite too.
You slight the source of mortals' fondest joys.
A marriage bed is mightier than oaths

when Fate approves and Justice sanctions it.
If you sleep sound when married partners kill,
exacting no revenge or punishment, 220
hunting Orestes can't be justified.
I know that you're incensed by certain crimes
and blatantly forgiving otherwise.
We'll go to trial! Let Pallas judge the case!

CORYPHAEUS:
I'll never let that criminal go free!

APOLLO:
Go chase him, then. Enjoy the extra work.

CORYPHAEUS:
Do not disparage honorable toil!

APOLLO:
I wouldn't choose to make such "honor" mine!

CORYPHAEUS:
But you're considered great by Zeus's throne,
while it's a mother's blood that's driving me. 230
I'll hound that man until there's justice done.

(Led by the CORYPHAEUS, the FURIES rush away
down a parodos. APOLLO steps forward, watches them
leave, and speaks before following them.)

APOLLO:
I'll aid my suppliant and rescue him,
for neither gods nor mortals like to face
the anger felt by suppliants betrayed.

The Holy Goddesses | 153

(The doors to APOLLO's temple close. The scene is now the temple of Athena Polias[16] on the Acropolis in Athens. The change of location is suggested by the crude wooden statue of ATHENA that has been discreetly placed on the stage. ORESTES enters via a parodos. He addresses the statue.)

ORESTES:
I've come, my queen, Athena, following
Apollo's orders. Grant this wanderer
a kind reception. I'm no suppliant
with bloody hands, just one who's worn away
and weary, traveling from house to house,
traversing land and sea alike to do   240
what Loxias's oracle advised.
I've reached the precinct where your image dwells.
I'll keep my vigil here awaiting trial.

(ORESTES sits by the statue with his hand on it as a way of claiming its protection. The CHORUS enters the orchēstra via the same parodos. They have been tracking ORESTES.)

CORYPHAEUS:
Well, well! We're clearly getting near the man.
Follow the trail of silent evidence.
His dripping blood will tell us where he's gone.
Like hounds, we'll flush and catch this wounded fawn.

16. The Parthenon's predecessor, the temple of Athena Polias (Athena of the City) was constructed in the 500s BCE and destroyed by the Persians in 480. It housed an ancient wooden cult statue that was said to have fallen from the sky. Work on the Parthenon did not begin until 447, eleven years after the first performance of the *Oresteia* in 458.

The Holy Goddesses

Slow down! My chest is heaving. All this work
would kill a mortal man! We've given chase
around the world, traversed the ocean like   250
a flock of wingless birds—outpacing ships.
And now our rabbit's cowering nearby.
Ah, the enticing smell of human blood!

(As the CHORUS reenters the orchēstra, each CHORISTER
sings or recites one or more verses.)

CHORISTER 1:
Look over these places again!   Choral Interlude (254–275)
Peruse the entire locale.
The matricide mustn't go free,
but if we're not careful he shall.

CHORISTER 2:
Oh, look! There he is!
What a confident smile,
embracing the goddess,
in hopes of a trial!

CHORISTER 3:
Impossible! For no maternal blood . . .

CHORISTER 4:
. . . that falls to earth can be restored.
It vanishes as soon as poured.

CHORISTER 5 (addressing ORESTES):
Your living self must pay us back with drink.

CHORISTER 6:
I'll take a draft of bitter brew,
the thick red blood that flows from you.

CHORISTER 7:
I'll lead you downward drained completely dry, . . .

CHORISTER 8:
. . . down below, where you'll be tried
and pay the price for matricide.

CHORISTER 9:
You'll witness every kind of sinner there, . . .

CHORISTER 10:
. . . those who disrespect the gods,
who treat their loving parents wrong
or cheat their hosts. For that's the place
where sinners such as those belong.

CHORISTER 11:
And each receives what Justice indicates,
for Hades is their great examiner,

CHORISTER 12:
the underground all-seeing lord,
who keeps a mental writing board,
on which he's careful to record
everything he sees.

ORESTES:
Amid my troubles I've been taught a host   276
of rituals, especially knowing when
it's time to speak and likewise when it's not.
And now it's time, or so my teacher says,
for blood that stained my fingers sleeps and fades.   280
The matricidal taint is washed away,
expelled, still fresh, by spilling piglets' blood,

cleansed by the holy hearth where Phoebus dwells.[17]
There isn't time for me to list all those
with whom I've later sojourned, harming none. 285
And now my pure and reverent prayer is that[18] 287
this nation's sovereign queen Athena come
to my assistance. Thus she'll peacefully
acquire me, my land, and Argive folk 290
as just and faithful friends forevermore.
Whether she's striding forth in Libya,[19]
assisting friends, or stands with covered feet[20]
by Triton's stream, where she was born and raised,[21]
or watches Phlegra's plain[22] as though she were
a mortal man, an army's dauntless chief,

17. Orestes claims that he has undergone rituals of purification at Delphi
and elsewhere. In some such rituals, the guilty party was showered with the
blood of a sacrificial piglet. The play does not seem to provide an opportunity
for Orestes to be purified at Delphi, from which he flees after line 93.

18. Line 286 ("Time as it ages cleanses everything") is deleted as an interpolation by Sommerstein and others on the grounds of irrelevance. It sounds
like a proverb originally written in the margin as a comparable sentiment.

19. An allusion to an Athenian expedition of two hundred ships sent to
Libya to assist the forces of a Libyan king rebelling against his and Egypt's
Persian masters. The expedition's chances for success apparently looked good
at the time that Aeschylus wrote the Oresteia. In the end, however, it was
destroyed by a Persian army with great loss of life. See Thucydides 1.104.1–2,
109.1–4.

20. Athena's gown covers her feet when she is standing still. When she is
"striding forth," her feet are uncovered.

21. Triton (trī'-tən) here is the god of the legendary northern African Lake
Tritonis, where some say Athena was born and raised. The story was invented
to explain Athena's mysterious Homeric title, Tritogeneia, "Triton-born."

22. Phlegra (fle'-grə), a peninsula (aka Pallene) projecting from northern
Greece. It is mentioned here as the site of the battle between the gods and the
giants. See Apollodorus 1.6.34–38.

may she—for gods can hear a distant prayer—
appear and be my liberator now.

CORYPHAEUS:
Neither Apollo nor Athena's strength
can rescue you. You'll roam forgotten, lost,   300
your heart bereft of every happiness,
a shade, the demons' bloodless nourishment.
What's that? Or don't you deign to answer me,
my consecrated fattened calf? You'll be
my living feast, and not a sacrifice.
Now lend your ears to our hypnotic song.

CHORUS:
Arise! Make a circle and dance!   Anapests (307–320)
The decision's been made to display
the art of our hate and explain
how we govern the fortunes of men.
We boast that we're utterly just.
Our anger is never unleashed
at those without blood on their hands.
They wander through life unimpaired.
But with secretive sinners like him,
his fingers still red from his crimes,
we testify, speaking for ghosts,
becoming the victims' avengers,
the final authority—ours!

You bore me, Mother Night,   Strophe 1 (321–327)
to punish those who err,
those blind or having sight,[23]

23. A way of saying the "the dead and the living."

but Leto's child[24] would dare
dishonor me by stealing
this man, this timid hare,
the sacrificial victim
we need in this affair.

Mad distractions, sorceries,   Mesode (328–333)
parching ills, cacophonies,
mind-enslaving melodies,
these are hymns Erinyes
sing at their sacrifice!

A hostile Fate decreed   Antistrophe 1 (334–340)
the burden we must bear:
all the mortal men
who purposefully dare
to spill a kinsman's blood
become our special care.
They don't escape in Hades.
We're present even there.

Mad distractions, sorceries,   Mesode (341–346)
parching ills, cacophonies,
mind-enslaving melodies,
these are hymns Erinyes
sing at their sacrifice!

Since birth it's been established   Strophe 2 (347–353)
we haven't any right
to touch divinities
or share an acolyte,

24. Apollo, son of Zeus and Leto (lē´-tō), daughter of the Titan Phoebe.

—or go to holy feasts
in robes of lily white.

We choose to level houses   Mesode (354–359)
reveling in sin,
when Ares turns domestic,
and someone murders kin.
However powerful
that person may have been,
we chase and apprehend him
and drain the blood within.

To spare the gods such labor   Antistrophe 2 (360–366)
we eagerly agree
to punish parricides.
We work so gods are free.
Zeus finds the bloodstained race
distasteful company.

The thoughts men have are grandiose   Strophe 3 (367–371)
      so long as skies are bright.
They wilt, however, underground,
      and all their pride takes flight
when they behold our angry dance
      and robes as dark as night.

I make a mighty leap,   Mesode (372–376)
landing on my toes,
all my weight behind them.
And down the runner goes!

What a disaster!

The fallen man does not know why.   Antistrophe 3 (377–380)
      His mind is quite undone.

Such is the dark, polluted cloud
*   that hovers over one.*
Sad rumors say that round his house
*   a fog obscures the sun.*

The clever and the consummate   Strophe 4 (381–388)
*   chroniclers of crime,*
whom mortal men cannot appease,
*   goddesses sublime,*
we work apart from other gods
*   in a filthy, sunless clime*
to roughen roads for men and ghosts,
*   and shall for all of time.*

Is there a man who doesn't feel   Antistrophe 4 (389–396)
*   a sense of awe and dread*
when, listening to me, he learns
*   what laws of fate have said*
about the ancient privilege
*   that I've inherited—*
although my duty's down below
*   where all the sunlight's fled.*

(ATHENA enters via a parodos.)

ATHENA:
I heard your distant cry for help in Troy   397
where I was marking off the plots of land
Achaean chiefs and leaders gave to me,
a liberal share of captured properties,   400
to be entirely mine eternally,
a gift to honor sons of Theseus.[25]

25. I.e., the Athenians.

From there I sped on unrelenting foot.
Instead of wings, my aegis[26] beat the air. 404
Now that I've seen this foreign company,[27] 406
I'm not afraid but marvel at the sight.
Say who you are. I'm asking all of you,
the stranger here, my statue's suppliant,
and you who don't resemble any kind 410
of god that visits us divinities,
nor do you look like normal human beings.
But speaking ill of passers-by who've done
no wrong is hardly just or civilized.

CORYPHAEUS:
I'll put it all concisely, Zeus's child.
We're Mother Night's eternal progeny.
They call us Curses underneath the earth.

ATHENA:
I know your parentage and title now.

CORYPHAEUS:
And soon you'll know our special honors too.

ATHENA:
If someone gives a clear account of them. 420

---

26. A magical goatskin cape fringed with serpents. In the *Iliad*, it belongs to Zeus. Holding it up and shaking it makes enemy armies panic (*Iliad* 17.593–596). In later literature and art, it is regularly worn by Athena.

27. Line 405 ("Young, eager ponies pulled my chariot") is deleted by Sommerstein, *Oresteia*, and others because it clearly contradicts lines 403–404. Evidently it was written for a production in which Athena entered by chariot rather than on "unrelenting foot."

CORYPHAEUS:
Our job is ridding homes of murderers.

ATHENA:
And where do exiled killers end their flight?

CORYPHAEUS:
A place where faring well is not the rule.

ATHENA:
Is that the journey you propose for him?

CORYPHAEUS:
He chose to be his mother's murderer!

ATHENA:
Was he compelled? Afraid of someone's wrath?

CORYPHAEUS:
What kind of fear excuses matricide?

ATHENA:
Two sides are here but only half the tale.

CORYPHAEUS:
He won't agree to our exchanging oaths.[28]

ATHENA:
You'd rather be *considered* just than be.   430

28. The Furies would swear that Orestes killed his mother. Orestes would then have the choice of swearing that he did not or conceding his guilt. There could be no consideration of extenuating circumstances.

CORYPHAEUS:
How's that? Explain. You're full of clever words.

ATHENA:
Injustice shouldn't win by swearing oaths.

CORYPHAEUS:
You try him, then, and make the verdict just.

ATHENA:
You'd really give the final word to me?

CORYPHAEUS:
Why not? It's fair. You're giving us our due.

ATHENA (addressing ORESTES):
Well, stranger, here's your chance to state your case.
Reveal your nation first, your parentage,
and what your troubles are, then your defense,
provided you're a pious suppliant
and keep a vigil near my sacred hearth   440
from trust in justice—not Ixion's[29] kind.
Give all my questions simple answers, please!

29. The story of Ixion (ik-sī´-ən) must be pieced together from various sources, especially Pindar, *Pythian* 2.17–48. It seems that he murdered his father-in-law, then successfully supplicated Zeus for purification. Zeus not only granted the request but allowed Ixion to join the gods in a feast on Olympus. There Ixion planned to seduce Hera. Learning his intention, Zeus made a facsimile of Hera out of a cloud, allowed Ixion to sleep with it, and then punished him: Ixion was attached to a wheel that rolled around the underworld endlessly while forced to proclaim the importance of gratitude. His son by the Hera-like cloud was Centaurus, who became the father of the centaurs by a group of mares. See further Timothy Gantz, *Early Greek Myth*, 2:718–20.

ORESTES:
My queen Athena, first I must remove
the worry that your latest words imply.
I'm no polluted suppliant. The hand
I clasp your image with is not defiled,
and I have cogent proof of this—to wit:
by law a violent killer may not speak
until a man adept at purges soaks
his head in blood that suckling piglets shed.   450
Now, bleeding beasts and flowing rivers cleansed
my head in other houses long ago.
And so I say that worry's out of place.
My family ties you'll recognize at once.
I'm Argive stock. You knew my father well.
His name was Agamemnon, king of ships.
With him you made a vacant lot of Troy,
but then he died ignobly back at home,
slain by my mother, heart as black as night.
She used his robes like cunning hunting nets.   460
His deadly bath had them as witnesses.
I spent some time in exile, then returned
and killed my mother. No, I don't deny
the deed. A father's death demands revenge.
Besides, Apollo's partially to blame,
for he foretold heartbreaking pains unless
I punished those responsible with death.
But was the killing just? That's up to you
to say. I will abide your ruling either way.

ATHENA:
This thing's too big for any mortal man.   470
It isn't even right for me to judge
a fiercely argued case of homicide,
especially since you've undergone those rites.
Yes, you're this house's pure and harmless suppliant,   474

but they have weighty privileges too.[30]   476
Unless a trial produces victory
for them, their venom might infect our soil
and leave our countryside forever ill.
So matters stand. To let you stay or not?   480
Each choice invites disaster. I'm perplexed.
But since this lightning bolt has landed here,   482
I'll choose a group of faultless citizens   475
to serve as murder judges, bound by vows   483
that I'll prescribe for now and future times.
But you assemble witnesses and proofs,
whatever helps to prove your plea is just.
I'll come when I've selected citizens
best qualified to judge the matter well,
without a broken oath or unjust thought.

(Exit ATHENA via a parodos.)

CHORUS:
Now, should this mother-killer's   Strophe 1 (490–498)
wrongful case succeed,
established laws will be
undone and mortals freed.

And there will be an age
of pure licentiousness.
Children striking parents
will often come of this.

No longer shall we maenads[31]   Antistrophe 1 (499–507)

---

30. The manuscript's line 475 is clearly out of place there. Sommerstein, *Oresteia*, and others transpose it to follow 482, where it fits perfectly.

31. Maenad (mē´-nad), a term applied to female followers of Dionysus and, secondarily, to any unnaturally excited women.

in anger seek to thwart
evils. We'll permit
deaths of every sort.

Alarmed by ills descending
on neighbors, men will seek
some end or some remission,
but their medicines are weak.

Then let nobody call on us,   Strophe 2 (508–516)
lamenting tragic injuries,
with cries and moans. "O Justice! O
majestic ones, Erinyes!"
For once the house of Justice falls,
you'll hear parental cries like these.

There are some times when fear is good.   Antistrophe 2 (517–525)
Its lofty duty's to review
human thinking. Virtue helps,
but where's the state or person who,
not brought up on fear, reveres
the Just as well as others do?

Avoid a life completely free,   Strophe 3 (526–537)
but don't submit to tyranny.
Though different governments are seen,
the gods put power in the mean.

And if a corollary's sought,
hubris comes from godless thought,
while joy, which all men hope to find,
is born of this: a healthy mind.

All in all my counsel is: Antistrophe 3 (538–549)
respect one altar: Justice's.

The Holy Goddesses | 167

Don't kick it down for godless gain.
You'll pay a price and feel the pain.

The end awaits and will be done.
In view of which, let everyone
revere his parents' holy name
and honor guests who bring him fame.

One freely just, not forced to be,   Strophe 4 (550–557)
is never ruined utterly.
His happiness is safe.

To him who boldly sails away
to unjust wealth, there comes a day,
a time to furl his sails.

Eventually a storm descends.
It tears the ragged sails and rends
the shattered yardarms too.

He calls on those who do not hear.   Antistrophe 4 (558–565)
The whirlpool's strong. He can't break clear.
His sweat amuses gods.

He thought that he would never be
buffeted so helplessly.
He can't surmount the waves.

His happy life has gone amiss.
He's crashed on reefs of righteousness,
and dies unwept, unseen.

(Enter ATHENA from the city, followed by a HERALD
and eleven citizens, her handpicked JURORS. During

the preceding choral song, stage furniture has been re-
arranged. The cult statue of Athena Polias is gone.
There are two urns for voting on a table, a throne for
ATHENA, and chairs for the JURORS. As ATHENA
reveals [line 685], the scene is now the Areopagus, not
the Acropolis.)

ATHENA:
Now do your duty, herald. Still the crowd.   566
Fill your Etruscan horn with mortal breath,
until its piercing voice divides the sky,
and every person hears its strident call.

(The HERALD produces a loud blast on his horn.
ATHENA sits on her throne.)

Now while this council chamber's filling up,   570
I ask these men and all the city too
to listen quietly while I explain
my timeless rules for seeing justice done.

(APOLLO enters abruptly, probably flying in on the
"machine.")

My lord Apollo! Rule your own domains!
Say what your purpose is in coming here.

APOLLO:
To be this person's witness, since he came,
a legal suppliant, to Delphi's hearth.
I washed the stains of murder off his hands.
I'll also be his advocate. I'll take
blame for his mother's death myself. But you   580
conduct the trial with all your knowledge now.

The Holy Goddesses | 169

ATHENA (addressing the CHORUS):
You have the floor. The trial's beginning now.
The prosecutor speaking first, from start
to finish, helps to clarify the case.

CHORUS:
As many as we are, we'll be concise.[32]

(Addressing ORESTES.)

Answer our questions point by point in turn.
First point: your mother—did you murder her?

ORESTES:
I killed her. Yes. There's no disputing that.

CHORUS:
Three falls in wrestling. One belongs to us.

ORESTES:
You boast too soon. I haven't fallen yet.   590

CHORUS:
Then tell us what your murder weapon was.

ORESTES:
A sword in hand, I cut my mother's throat.

CHORUS:
And who or what persuaded you to act?

---

32. This line seems to imply that, contrary to the usual practice, the
whole chorus speaks in unison without musical accompaniment.

ORESTES:
This god's prophetic words. He'll vouch for me.

CHORUS:
His prophet recommended matricide?

ORESTES:
So far, at least, I'd call his guidance good.

CHORUS:
If you're convicted, you'll revise your view.

ORESTES:
I'm not afraid. My father's ghost will help.

CHORUS:
The mother-killer trusts in corpses now!

ORESTES:
She bore the stains of two disgusting sins.   600

CHORUS:
Two sins? How so? Instruct the judges, please!

ORESTES:
She killed a spouse and killed a father—mine.

CHORUS:
Her death acquitted her, but you're alive!

ORESTES:
In life you didn't bother her. Why not?

CHORUS:
Her victim wasn't joined to her by blood.

ORESTES:
And I? Do I contain my mother's blood?

CHORUS:
Her womb was your provider, murderer!
Would you deny the bond of mother's blood?

ORESTES:
Your turn, Apollo. Set the matter straight.
In killing her, did I do right or wrong?   610
I don't deny the killing. That's a fact.
But you must judge the bloodshed just or not
so I can tell this jury what you say.

APOLLO:
To you and great Athena's court I say:
the deed was justly done. I won't defile
my mantic throne with lies. Concerning men,
women, and cities, I proclaim the truths
that heaven's father Zeus reveals through me.
Consider what a powerful defense
that is, and bend to Zeus's will. No oath   620
you may have taken weighs as much as that.

CHORUS:
So Zeus told you to tell Orestes here
to massacre his father's murderers,
but freely disregard his mother's rights?

APOLLO:
Their cases aren't the same. A noble man
who bore a scepter given him by Zeus
fell by a woman. Not an Amazon.
She didn't shoot far-darting shafts at him.

You'll hear the facts, Athena; as will you,
you men who've gathered here to cast your votes.   630
The king had just returned from waging war
and doing rather well. She greeted him
with cheerful words and watched while he enjoyed
(a steaming bath that filled a silver tub,)[33]
but then she threw a garment over him,
an ornate robe and husband-trap, and struck.
And so the person died the way I've said,
that most majestic man, the king of ships.
In speaking as I have, I hope I've stung
the people authorized to judge this case.

CHORUS:
You say a father's death means more to Zeus.   640
He chained his aged father, Cronus, once![34]
Are not those statements contradictory?
I beg the judges: make a note of that.

APOLLO:
You loathsome monsters whom the gods detest!
It's possible to loosen chains. The cure
is there. Escape has many tools to choose,
but once the dust absorbs a mortal's blood,
there isn't any way to make him rise.
My father hasn't made a charm for that.

33. A line has dropped out of the manuscript here. My translation is
based on Sommerstein, *Oresteia*, 434 n. 130.

34. In Hesiod's *Theogony* 711–720, Zeus and the Olympians overthrow
the Titans with the help of hundred-armed giants. When victory is secured,
they chain the Titans, including Zeus's father, Cronus (krō´-näs), in the depths
of Tartarus.

The Holy Goddesses | 173

All other states he alters easily,   650
reversing them by force of will alone.

CHORUS:
It's strange that you'd defend this person, then.
He spilled maternal blood, the same as his.
Where will he live? In Argos? Occupy
his father's house? Use the altars there?
What phratry[35] wouldn't shut their doors on him?

APOLLO:
I'll tell you. Here's my flawless argument.
A so-called mother's not a parent. No.
She's but a nurse, the seedling embryo's.
Who mounts begets. The female just protects   660
the sprouts that heaven spares like foreign guests.
Fathers give birth without a mother's help.
I'll offer you decisive proof of that.
She's standing there: Athena, Zeus's child.[36]
She wasn't nursed in any pitch-dark womb,
this child the like of which no goddess bore.

(Addressing ATHENA.)

Pallas, I'll make your town and army great
in different ways within my competence,
mostly by sending you this suppliant

35. A phratry or brotherhood was an hereditary subgroup of the population of Athens and many other city-states. One could not be a citizen without
admission to a phratry.

36. Athena was born from Zeus's forehead: the reason for the ectopic
pregnancy was that he had impregnated Metis, Wisdom personified, and
swallowed her, fearing her offspring (Hesiod, *Theogony* 886–900).

to be your faithful friend for all of time,
both him and his descendants, loyal friends
and allies too; that way these faithful oaths
will always please your judges' progeny.

ATHENA:
Is now the time to cast your honest votes?
Have I allowed sufficient time for talk?

APOLLO:
My every shaft's already shot. The game
is done. I'm waiting now to learn who won.

ATHENA (addressing the CHORUS):
And you? Can I escape your censure too?

CHORUS (addressing the JURORS):
The arguments already heard suffice.
In voting let your hearts respect your oath.

ATHENA:
People of Athens, first to try a man
for murder, hear the law that I propose.
In future days, the tribe of Aegeus[37]
shall always hold a jurors' council here,
the rugged peak where Amazons made camp
when they attacked, resenting Theseus,[38]
and built a second citadel, a fort

670

680

---

37. Aegeus (ē´-jē-əs), Theseus' father. His "sons" are the Athenians.

38. Athenian mythology included an invasion of the city by Amazons, who were repelled with great difficulty. No complete, canonical version of the story survives. All agree that Theseus caused the war by running off with the Amazon queen Antiope.

whose towers rivaled our Acropolis.
They prayed to Ares then, and so we named
that rugged peak the Areopagus.   690
Here citizens' respect and inborn fear
will extirpate injustice night and day—
provided they refrain from changing laws.
For water once defiled by mud and filth
no longer satisfies a person's thirst.
I urge your leading men to love the state
that's neither anarchy nor tyranny
and not to banish every sort of dread.
What mortal man is just who knows no fear?
By fearing such a sacred court as this,   700
you'll gain a fort protecting land and town—
a fort the like of which nobody owns
in Scythia[39] or where lord Pelops[40] ruled.
This council—incorruptible, august,
indignant—I declare that it shall be
this nation's wakeful guard when others sleep.
I hope in days to come this lengthy speech
will benefit my fellow citizens.
Now rise and, gathering your pebbles, vote.
Respect your oaths. I've nothing more to say.   710

CORYPHAEUS:
As your advisor, my advice is this:
Do not offend our dangerous company.

39. Scythia (si´-thē-ə), a barbarian land covering much of Eastern Europe
and Central Asia.
40. Pelops (pe´-läps), the son of Tantalus, father of Atreus and Thyestes,
king of Pisa, the area around Olympia.

The Holy Goddesses

(As the CORYPHAEUS speaks, the first JUROR votes by
dropping a pebble into the jar labeled "guilty.")

APOLLO:
I say to fear prophetic words from Zeus
and me. They mustn't wither unfulfilled.

(The second JUROR votes "innocent.")

CORYPHAEUS:
You're judging bloody deeds. That's not your role.
Soon they'll pollute your holy oracle.

(The third JUROR votes "guilty.")

APOLLO:
Then I suppose my father acted wrong.
He cleansed Ixion, man's first murderer.

(The fourth JUROR votes "innocent.")

CORYPHAEUS:
Perhaps, but if the verdict isn't just,
this countryside will feel my crushing weight.   720

(The fifth JUROR votes "guilty.")

APOLLO:
The older gods and younger ones refuse
to honor you. My victory's assured.

(The sixth JUROR votes "innocent.")

The Holy Goddesses | 177

CORYPHAEUS:
Your deeds in Pheres' house were lawless too![41]
Seducing Fates to rescue men from death!

(The seventh JUROR votes "guilty.")

APOLLO:
To benefit a pious suppliant,
especially one in need—is that not just?

(The eighth JUROR votes "innocent.")

CORYPHAEUS:
But you corrupted primal deities
beguiling ancient goddesses with wine.

(The ninth JUROR votes "guilty.")

APOLLO:
You'll quickly lose your suit and realize
your venom doesn't hurt your enemies.   730

(The tenth JUROR votes "innocent.")

---

41. Euripides' *Alcestis* is the earliest surviving version of the relevant myth. Pheres' (fer´-ēz) son, Admetus, is a king befriended by Apollo. When Apollo learns that Admetus is destined to die young, he persuades the three Fates to let Admetus off the hook—if he can find a replacement to die for him. Aeschylus is the earliest source for the detail that Apollo used wine to soften up the Fates. Admetus canvasses all of his friends, but only his wife, Alcestis, agrees to help him. In Euripides' version, the story ends happily. As Death tries to take Alcestis to the underworld, Admetus' friend Heracles intervenes, defeats Death in a wrestling match, and restores her alive to her husband.

The Holy Goddesses

CORYPHAEUS:
Despite my age, you've disrespected me,
young god. I'll stay to hear the verdict read
and maybe make your city feel my wrath.

(The eleventh JUROR votes "guilty.")

ATHENA:
It falls to me to cast the final vote.
I vote in favor of Orestes. Why?
No woman had a role in bearing me.
Apart from marriage, I embrace the male
in everything. I'm quite my father's child.
Therefore, a woman's death, especially one
who killed her spouse, is valued less by me.   740

(ATHENA votes "innocent.")

If votes are tied, the man accused prevails.
You judges, those to whom the job's assigned,
empty the jars that hold the ballots now!

ORESTES:
Phoebus Apollo, how's the trial to end?

CORYPHAEUS:
Dark Night, our mother, be our witness now!

ORESTES:
My end's a deadly noose or light of day.

CORYPHAEUS:
We'll see our honors grow or go astray.

The Holy Goddesses | 179

APOLLO:
Be careful counting ballots, gentlemen,
and be completely fair to all concerned.
Great harm is often done by carelessness.   750
A single vote can save a falling house.

> (As APOLLO finishes speaking, ATHENA receives a tally
> sheet from a JUROR.)

ATHENA:
The man's found innocent of spilling blood,
for equal votes were cast on either side.

> (Exit APOLLO flying.)

ORESTES:
O Pallas, you've restored my house and home.
My father's land was lost. You brought it back.
Now some Hellenic fellow's bound to say:
"The man's an Argive once again and rules
his father's land by Pallas's decree
with Loxias, and, third, the savior, Zeus"—
my savior, who avenged my father's death   760
by facing down my mother's advocates.
I'm going home. Before I do, I'll swear
by this your land and these your people here
that armored men who steer our ship of state
shall never start a war against your land
in all the twists and turns of future time.
Though I'll be dead and buried then myself,
I'll send upon whoever violates
my oath misfortunes lacking remedy.
I'll watch them losing heart on journeys, scared   770
by evil signs till they regret their steps.

But if they always honor Athens well
with allied force and keep my oaths intact,
I'll prove to be a very gracious friend.
Goddess, farewell! And men of Athens too!
Your adversaries can't escape your grip.
You'll always be victorious and safe.

(Exit ORESTES via a parodos. The JURORS stay on
their benches watching the CHORUS and reacting
appropriately to the spectacle.)

CHORUS:

Young gods, you tread on ancient laws!　　　Strophe 1 (778–793)
You stole my rights by sleight of hand!
I'm disrespected, wretched, mad.
You'll see my poison soak your land,
a barren rain infecting earth.
You'll see it spread across the plain,
a leafless canker (Justice, hear!),
bringing mortals deadly pain.
I weep, but what is there to do?
I'm mocked. My will is always crossed.
We're luckless daughters born of Night,
grieving over honors lost.

ATHENA:

Hear me and stop your lamentation now.　　　794
You didn't lose. The votes were tied. There's no
dishonor there. I'm telling you the truth.
The evidence of Zeus's will was clear.
Besides, his prophet told us this himself:
Orestes shouldn't suffer any harm
for what he did. So spare the Attic earth　　　800
your crushing wrath. Control your temper. Don't

create sterility with breaths that leave
a ghastly froth devouring our seeds.
I promise absolutely that you'll have
abodes and secret chambers all your own.
You'll sit enthroned by luminescent hearths,
accepting honors citizens bestow.

CHORUS:
Young gods, you tread on ancient laws!   Antistrophe 1 (808–823)
You stole my rights by sleight of hand!
I'm disrespected, wretched, mad.
You'll see my poison soak your land,
a barren rain infecting earth.
You'll see it spread across the plain,
a leafless canker (Justice, hear!),
bringing mortals deadly pain.
I weep but what is there to do?
I'm mocked. My will is always crossed.
We're luckless daughters born of Night,
grieving over honors lost.

ATHENA:
You're not dishonored, goddesses. Be calm!   824
Don't change the mortals' land to barren waste.
Zeus stands behind my words. Why mention that
or say that I'm the only god who knows
the chest in which his lightning bolts are locked?
No need! Be kind. Don't issue empty threats
against the earth, as though whatever bears   830
a fruit of any sort must surely die.
No! Let your dark and bitter mood subside.
Become my neighbor, honored reverently.
Once you've received this spacious land's first fruits,
and gifts that brides and pregnant women give,
you'll never finish praising my advice.

CHORUS:

To think that I must suffer so!   Strophe 2 (837–847)
Ancient wisdom hides below,
like something decent men detest.
Violent fury fills my chest.
Mother Night, are you aware
of all the pain that I must bear?
These trickster gods are truly deft.
They stole my honors. Nothing's left.

ATHENA:

I'll bear your anger patiently. You're old.   848
Older than me and therefore wiser far,
but Zeus has given me some wisdom too.   850
Go! Find another country. I predict
you'll soon be missing this one horribly.
The passing age will bring these citizens
increasing honors. You yourself would have
a special place beside Erechtheus[42]
and win from male and female votaries
such gifts as mortals never gave before.
Just don't implant in places loved by me
whatever whets a thirst for blood and fills
young minds with passions not produced by wine.   860
Don't put the hearts of fighting cockerels
in peaceful citizens, inciting them
to tribal violence, internecine war.
Let foreign wars rage on, enough to sate
the man who knows the urgent love of fame!
Avoid the kind domestic fowls conduct.
Such is the sort of life I offer you:

42. Erechtheus (ar-rek´-thē-əs), an early mythical king of Athens worshipped on the Acropolis with Athena.

do good; be prosperous, honored well;
and join the nation most beloved by gods.

CHORUS:
To think that I must suffer so!   Antistrophe 2 (869–880)
Ancient wisdom hides below,
like something decent men detest.
Violent fury fills my chest.
Mother Night, are you aware
of all the pain that I must bear?
These trickster gods are truly deft.
They've robbed my honors. Nothing's left.

ATHENA:
I'll never tire speaking well of you.   881
You'll never say that I, a younger god,
and these my citizens permitted you
to wander here disgraced without a home.
So if Persuasion's force compels respect
and if my tongue is good at casting spells,
you'll stay. But even if you still refuse,
you haven't any reason to direct
your anger, wrath, or injuries at them.
Some of this country could belong to you,   890
and you'd be honored here eternally.

CORYPHAEUS:
What sort of home are you proposing, then?

ATHENA:
One missing only misery. Give in!

CORYPHAEUS:
Suppose I do, what honor waits for me?

ATHENA:
No house will flourish absent your consent.

CORYPHAEUS:
You'll see that power such as that is mine?

ATHENA:
We'll heal your worshippers' misfortunes too.

CORYPHAEUS:
Will I receive your solemn pledge on that?

ATHENA:
I don't indulge in empty promises.

CORYPHAEUS:
You're charming me. My anger's fading now.   900

ATHENA (speaking with finality):
In other words, you'll stay and make new friends.

CORYPHAEUS:
What blessings should the spells I cast produce?

ATHENA:
Only those blessings not ignobly won:
the gifts the earth and seaborne foam provide;
the gentle breaths of breezes heaven-sent
that waft across the land on sunny days;
abundant fruits of earth and roaming herds
so large they'll never fail the citizens.
Preserve the seeds of mortal men as well.
Grant pious folk increased fertility.   910
I cherish like a careful gardener

the happy race of these fair-minded men.
Such peaceful matters though are your concern.
I won't refrain from wars where glory's won.
I'll make this city famed for victories.

CHORUS:
I'll live with Pallas lest I slight   Strophe 1 (916–926)
the city Zeus, almighty lord,
and Ares made the gods' delight,
and guard of shrines where they're adored.

Hear my happy prophecies!
The sun will make the good earth grow
all of life's necessities
and other blessings row on row.

ATHENA:
I'm doing my townsfolk a favor   Anapests (927–937)
by settling these goddesses here,
hard to appease though they be.
They manage all human affairs.
The man they encounter when angry
is beaten and doesn't know why.
His ancestors' sins are the reason.
He's led to the goddesses' court,
boasting out loud all the way.
Then silent destruction descends:
The goddesses' anger's at work.

CHORUS:
No winds will come that hurt your trees,   Antistrophe 1 (938–948)
nor fiery breaths that kill buds blow
inside your lands with their disease.
Such are the favors I bestow.

Let Pan have healthy rams and ewes
bearing twins as time unwinds.
Let earth-rich generations choose,
repaying the gods for lucky finds.[43]

ATHENA (addressing the JURORS):
City's defense, do you hear
what their words are accomplishing now?
The Furies have absolute powers
among the immortals and those
who are under the earth; and their actions
on humans are easily seen.
For some they deliver a life
that's like a melodious song;
for others, a life full of tears.

Anapests (949–955)

CHORUS:
I ban untimely deaths of men.
Give lovely girls their married bliss!
O sister Fates, apportioners,
the power's yours to grant all this.
You play a part in every house.
How weighty your assistance is,
protecting righteous human bonds,
most highly honored goddesses!

Strophe 2 (956–967)

ATHENA:
I rejoice in the goddesses' kindness,

Anapests (968–975)

43. A "lucky find" is a *hermaion,* literally "a gift from Hermes," the god associated with good luck. The verse probably alludes to the lucky discovery of rich veins of silver at Laurium. In the 480s profits were used providentially to build up the Athenian fleet in advance of the Persian invasion. Defeating the Persians is how the Athenians paid the gods back.

to promise so much for my land,
and I cherish the smiles of Persuasion,
which guided my lips and my tongue
when facing indignant rejection.
Zeus of the Agora won[44]—
Zeus and my struggle for goodness,
enduring forever.

CHORUS:

May civil strife that never gets   Antistrophe 2 (976–987)
its fill of grief not thunder here.
Don't let our dust turn black with blood
or think exchange of murders dear
from too much love of punishment.
Receiving joys, reciprocate
and note that many evils find
a remedy in common hate.

ATHENA:

Does it sound like they mean to discover   Anapests (988–995)
the paths of beneficent speech?
You townsmen will benefit greatly
from fear of their frightening looks.
By returning their kindness and honors,
you'll govern the city more justly
and gather eternal renown.

CHORUS:

Rejoice in wealth that's moderate,   Strophe 3 (996–1002)
dear Athenians who sit

---

44. I.e., Zeus of the Assembly Place. There was a statue of Zeus in the Athenian Agora, but this is Athena's way of crediting her success to discussion and debate.

near Zeus's favorite child,
who dwell beneath Athena's wings[45]
with wisdom time in passing brings,
and Zeus himself reveres you.

ATHENA (addressing the FURIES):
Join the rejoicing yourselves!   Anapests (1003–1013)
I'll show you the way to your chambers.

> (The SECOND CHORUS enters from the skēnē, which
> now represents the temple of ATHENA on the Acropolis.
> The SECOND CHORUS consists of the priestess of
> ATHENA and her entourage of acolytes, young and old.
> Some carry torches; others, purple robes. One escorts a
> pair of sacrificial animals, lambs perhaps.)

These escorts will brighten your way.
And once you have entered the earth,
and the blood of these victims is spilt,
keep everything harmful to Athens
under the ground, but release
whatever is good for the city
and crowns it with victory wreaths.

> (To the SECOND CHORUS.)

Cranaus's[46] children, born in the city,
show recent arrivals the way.

---

45. Possibly a reference to a statue of Athena that identified her with
Nikē, victory personified, a winged goddess normally thought of as Athena's
companion.

46. Cranaus (krä-nā´-əs), like Erechtheus an early, mythical king of
Athens. Translated to English, his name is "Rocky."

The Holy Goddesses | 189

(To the JURORS.)

And citizens, see that your thoughts
are as good as the good that's occurred.

CHORUS:
Rejoice! Rejoice! Again! Again!   Antistrophe 3 (1014–1020)
immortal gods and mortal men
in Pallas's community.

If you accept my presence here
piously, you needn't fear
that grief will mar your life.

ATHENA:
I like the sound of that majestic vow,   1021
but now I'll usher you, while torches light
the way, to chambers underneath the ground.
My statue's guardians will lend a hand,
and rightly.

(She addresses the SECOND CHORUS, which enters
the orchēstra as ATHENA speaks. Some drape their
purple robes over the FURIES' black gowns. Others
holding torches take positions near a parodos. They are
preparing to lead the CHORUS and others offstage to
the FURIES' new underground chambers.)

Jewel of Theseus' land,[47]
go forth, distinguished company of girls,

47. The text is riddled with problems here. I follow A. J. Podlecki's
edition of *Eumenides* in treating the "jewel" of Athens as a reference to its
women, as symbolized by the chorus of Athena's attendants. According to

and band of reverend matrons young and old!
Honor these goddesses by cloaking them
in purple robes,[48] then let your torches shine!
That way they'll always be our friends, renowned   1030
for blessing us with manly excellence.

SECOND CHORUS (leading the FURIES to their
          underground chambers):

O great, ambitious, childless progeny   Strophe 1 (1032–1035)
of Mother Night, come down the path with me,
your friendly escort. Silence, countrymen!

Beneath the depths of earth, the state   Antistrophe 1 (1036–1038)
          decrees,
you'll be our sacrifices' honorees,
revered uniquely. Silence, citizens!

Holy Goddesses,[49] be gracious   Strophe 2 (1039–1043)
          and kindly come below.
Enjoy the flaming torches
          we carry as we go.
O-lo-lu-gay!

Sommerstein in his Loeb edition (note 195) the "jewel" in question is the
Acropolis, which in his view is the procession's destination: "Come forth to
the jewel of Athens."

48. Such robes were worn by resident aliens in religious processions.
Thus they symbolize the official inclusion of the goddesses in the state.

49. The term *Eumenides* does not occur anywhere in the play, and it is
doubtful that it had become a euphemism for the Furies (Greek *Erinyes*) at
the time this play was written. This line identifies the reformed Furies with
the mysterious "Holy Goddesses" (*Semnai*) who had a sanctuary in or near a
cave at the foot of the Areopagus.

The Holy Goddesses

This peace will last forever.[50]   Antistrophe 2 (1044–1047)
    Omniscient Zeus and Fate
combine to guard Athena's
    belovéd city-state.
O-lo-lu-gay!

50. Line 1044 is unintelligible as transmitted. My restoration is based on the fact that it contains words for "truce" and possibly "forever." The rest of the stanza envisions the beneficial cooperation of the older gods (e.g., Fate) and the newer Olympians (e.g., Zeus).

Appendix 1

Synopses

Aeschylus' dramatic trilogy, the *Oresteia*, concerns the family of Agamemnon, king of Argos and conqueror of Troy. The first play is *Agamemnon*. With its bold metaphors, unremitting irony, and pervasive suspense, it is the *Hamlet* of ancient Greece's dramatic poetry. As the play begins, word reaches Clytaemestra, wife of the absent Agamemnon, that Troy has fallen. She claims to be jubilant, but hints abound that her real feelings are different. We have learned why that might be so through a flashback in the opening choral song. When Agamemnon was setting sail for Troy, he sacrificed his and Clytaemestra's daughter Iphigeneia to the goddess Artemis to get fair winds for the voyage.

Back in the present, Agamemnon arrives from Troy. He is accompanied by his "prize," the Trojan princess and prophetess Cassandra. Clytaemestra persuades her husband to enter his palace by trampling a purple tapestry, a hubristic act calculated to incur resentment, human and divine.

Clytaemestra tells Cassandra to come in too, in order to participate in a sacrifice, but Cassandra refuses until she has prophesied one last time. In a long lyrical passage, she predicts Agamemnon's imminent murder and her own in veiled terms to the chorus of elders. They are slow to grasp her meaning.

Soon after she enters the palace (or, in her words, the slaughterhouse), Agamemnon's cry is heard: "*Omoi!* I'm struck a fatal blow within." The chorus doesn't know what, if anything, they should do. At last they agree that they need to know exactly what has happened. As though to oblige them, the palace doors open to reveal the bloodstained queen standing over the bodies of Agamemnon and Cassandra. Far from being remorseful, she boasts about striking her husband repeatedly as he reclined in his bath. She adds this:

> he vomited a shining clot of blood,
> which dappled me with dark red drops of dew.
> It made me glad, as glad as farmers' fields
> when thanks to god the blossoms start to bloom.
>
> (1389–1392)

She also declares that killing Cassandra was a kind of dessert.

The rest of the play is devoted to the confrontation between Clytaemestra and the chorus of horrified elders. At first she takes full credit for the murders, justifying them by reference to the sacrifice of Iphigeneia. As her passions cool, however, she assigns more responsibility to the ghosts of other past murder victims who still haunt the palace. In fact, she reveals that she relies on the protection of Agamemnon's ancient enemy Aegisthus, whose brothers were killed by Agamemnon's father in the course of a bloody internecine feud. On cue, Aegisthus himself enters the scene, delighted by the murder of Agamemnon. Although Clytaemestra did the killing, Aegisthus boasts that he did the planning. He and the chorus nearly come to blows, but Clytaemestra finally prevails on everyone to leave calmly: the chorus to their homes, she and Aegisthus to the palace. She hopes there will be no more bloodshed.

The next two plays in the trilogy, *Libation Bearers* and *Eumenides*, lack *Agamemnon*'s magnificent poetry but make up for it with a hallucinatory quality that casts its own peculiar spell.

Libation Bearers reminds the audience that Agamemnon's son, Orestes, has been raised in a different kingdom, ostensibly to keep him safe while his father was at Troy. Now he returns to Argos at Apollo's command to avenge his father's murder by killing his mother as well as her partner in crime, Aegisthus. Orestes arrives in Argos at a spot near his father's grave. There he sees his sister Electra and a chorus of elderly slave women bringing libations to pour on the dead king's grave. Once they have done so, Orestes reveals himself to Electra. Their emotional reunion leads to an extraordinarily long choral passage (lines 315–478) in which they lament their father's death and pray to his spirit for help.

As if to compensate for its slow beginning, the rest of the play is, by the standards of Greek tragedy, packed with action. Orestes pretends to be a stranger bringing the news that a fellow named Orestes has died. Clytaemestra claims to be saddened, though one never knows. She invites the disguised Orestes to spend the night and sends for Aegisthus. He arrives hurriedly to interview the stranger himself, saying that he won't be misled by a mere rumor. As he enters the palace, the chorus chants ominously until they are interrupted by an effeminate cry: "*Eee! Eee! Otótotoi!*" A panic-stricken servant emerges from the palace. The master has been killed, he cries, and Clytaemestra's life is in danger!

Clytaemestra enters and demands to know what is happening. She reacts with typical boldness:

> Bring me a lethal weapon! Get an ax!
> We'll either win or lose. So let's find out!
> I've finally reached the peak of misery.

> (889–891)

She never gets a weapon, though. Orestes arrives first with sword drawn and orders her to go inside the palace so that he can kill her beside her lover. She pleads for her life, even baring her breast to win her son's sympathy, but to no avail. She meekly enters the palace. After a choral interlude, the palace doors open to reveal Orestes standing over his victims. The chorus congratulates him on liberating the land from a tyranny, but Orestes is not in a mood to be congratulated. He feels that he is losing his mind. Furies, dreadful snake-haired goddesses from the underworld, are coming to get him. He cannot stay! He runs offstage, heading for Delphi and Apollo's protection. The chorus wishes him luck and wonders whether the family's cycle of violence will ever end.

Eumenides begins outside Apollo's temple at Delphi. His priestess, the Pythia, says her morning prayers and enters the temple to prepare for the day's business. For a few long moments, the stage and orchestra are empty. Then the Pythia comes rushing out on hands and knees, horrified. The inner shrine is occupied by sleeping Furies and a desperate suppliant with a bloody sword. The Pythia runs off, saying that Apollo himself has to deal with the situation.

The temple doors open on the scene that the Pythia described. The suppliant is Orestes, who prays to Apollo for help. The god appears, takes credit for putting the Furies to sleep, and tells Orestes that he must hurry to Athens. There Athena will conduct a trial in which he will be vindicated and liberated from the Furies. Orestes runs off as directed.

Inside the temple, the ghost of Clytaemestra appears and angrily urges the Furies to wake up. Eventually they do. Being this play's chorus, they come streaming out of the temple, singing and dancing, and take up positions in the orchestra. Meanwhile, Clytaemestra's ghost sneaks away, and Apollo steps forward again. At the end of the Furies' song, he orders them to leave. They object that they are just doing their job: chasing those who spill kindred blood. Apollo declares that Athena will settle the case. Promising that they will never give up the chase, the Furies rush off after Orestes.

Again the stage and orchestra are briefly empty. A change of scene is indicated by the presence of a statue of Athena. The setting is now her temple on the Athenian Acropolis. Orestes enters and prays to Athena for help.

The Furies enter. They have been tracking Orestes, following the scent of blood. They perform a long ode condemning him and describing their own awesome powers.

> We choose to level houses
> reveling in sin,
> when Ares turns domestic
> and someone murders kin.
> However powerful
> that person may have been,
> we chase and apprehend him
> and drain the blood within.
>
> (354–359)

Athena arrives as the song ends. She listens to both sides and declares the case too difficult for any mortal mind or even her own to decide. Instead, she will select a group of citizens to act as a jury. She leaves to recruit them.

While they await Athena's return, the chorus favors the audience with another long ode. This time their theme is that injustice would run rampant if weren't for fear of the Furies.

Athena returns with eleven citizens and is starting to lay down the rules for the trial when Apollo appears. He has come as a witness to the fact that Orestes was purified at Delphi and as his advocate.

Both sides present their arguments. The Furies maintain that Orestes spilled kindred blood by killing his mother. Apollo argues that children are not related by blood to their mothers, whose wombs are just temporary receptacles. The proof is Athena herself, born from Zeus's forehead without a mother.

When the human votes are cast, six favor condemnation,

five acquittal. Athena has the last vote. She declares that a tie vote will work in favor of the defendant and votes to acquit Orestes, explaining that she favors the male since she did not have a mother. Orestes is freed by the tie vote.

Orestes returns happily to Argos, saying that that city will always be friendly with Athens. The Furies, however, are outraged and threaten to poison Athens' fields.

Athena takes it upon herself to win them over. As they sing their angry threats and complaints, she offers them an underground home in Athens where they will be honored and receive rich sacrifices. At last, their anger is overcome by her generosity and tact. They sing about the many blessings that they will heap on the Athenians.

At the very end of the play, Athena summons a second chorus consisting of her own priestess and other acolytes. They replace the Furies' black rags with purple robes and lead them to their new homes under the earth, where they will be known not as the ill-omened "Furies" but as the "Holy Goddesses."

Appendix 2

Aeschylus' Biography

The manuscripts of Aeschylus' plays include an ancient anonymous biography of the poet. *Suda*, a Byzantine encyclopedia, contains a much shorter version. These sources contain two kinds of material. First, there is chronological information about Aeschylus' life and the highlights of his career. Scholars deem this material to be largely reliable. Much of it derives from records kept by Athenian magistrates of yearly winners of the dramatic competitions at the springtime festival known as the Great Dionysia or the City Dionysia. Some of those records, called *didaskaliai,* still survive, literally carved in stone.[1] Others were copied by Aristotle and passed on via his writings to the scholars of Alexandria and their heirs.

The other sort of material found in those biographies and other ancient sources consists of colorful anecdotes that are anything but reliable. It is not the work of scientific biographers. Apart from the archons' records and Aristotle's research, what we have are the kind of apocryphal tales that grow up around celebrities in the absence of documentation.

Ancient Greek biographers assumed that people reached the height of their powers at the age of forty. Hence, they guessed birth years by subtracting forty from the year of a person's first outstanding achievement. In Aeschylus' case, that was his first victory at the Great Dionysia, which occurred in 484 BCE. To this day, therefore, his year of birth is given as "circa 525/524," which fits well with the genuinely datable events in his life. If it is correct, he began to compose dramas as a relatively young man. At the Great Dionysia, competing dramatists presented tetralogies: three tragedies and a farcical satyr play. Aeschylus' first tetralogy was produced in 499, when, by the forty-year rule, he would have been in his mid-twenties. He did not, however, enjoy early success as a playwright. He was in his mid-thirties, still uncrowned, in 490 when the invading Persians landed in superior numbers at Marathon and were driven into the sea by brave Athenian hoplites, probably including Aeschylus himself.

His first winning tetralogy was produced six years later, in 484. There is reason to think that it included a play called *Myrmidons*[2] that dramatized the heart of the *Iliad*: the death of Patroclus and Achilles' great sorrow. The play began with Odysseus and Phoenix trying to persuade a silent, shrouded Achilles to rejoin the battle against the Trojans. Several vase paintings from the period depict that scene and could be a testimony to the popularity of Aeschylus' play.[3] A surviving fragment of the play shows that Aeschylus departed from Homer's version to depict the two heroes as homosexual lovers.[4] That touch may have helped secure its fame. In any event, from 484 forward Aeschylus was Athens' leading dramatist, winning a dozen more victories in twenty-five years.

The early years of Aeschylus' dominance in the theater were marked by the great battles of Salamis (480) and Plataea (479), in which Persia's land and sea invasion of Greece came to grief. The earliest of his extant plays, *Persians*, is a celebration of those Greek victories and was part of a winning tetralogy. Depicting the distress in the Persian court in the wake of Salamis, it was produced in 472 with the young Pericles as *choregus*—that is, the sponsor who bore the costs of the production, chiefly the expense of training the chorus. At the heart of the play is a description of the battle of Salamis by a grief-stricken Persian messenger.

Aeschylus suffered a setback in the Great Dionysia of 468, beaten by the young Sophocles, who was competing for the first time. We do not know the titles of Aeschylus' plays for that year. Sophocles' winners included *Triptolemus*, a story about the hero who spread Demeter's gift, the knowledge of growing grain, around the world.

In 467 Aeschylus recovered and took another first prize with a tetralogy about the family of Oedipus. The surviving play, *Seven against Thebes*, dramatizes moments from the mythical civil war between Eteocles and Polyneices, the sons of King Oedipus, for control of the city of Thebes. In the central passage, Eteocles listens to a messenger describing the stupendous warriors under Polyneices' command who are preparing to attack the city's seven gates. Eteocles then appoints a Theban defender to fight each one. The seventh rebel captain named is his own brother, Polyneices. Over the chorus's objections, Eteocles volunteers to fight Polyneices himself and marches off to do battle. After a choral song, word arrives that the other defenders were victorious but the battle between Eteocles and Polyneices was a draw: they killed each other.

Aeschylus' *Suppliants* was produced around the same time as *Seven against Thebes*. The suppliants of the title are fifty sisters of Greek ancestry who grew up in Egypt but fled to Greece to avoid being married against their wills to their fifty Egyptian cousins. Little happens in the extant play. The good Greek king agrees to protect the maidens, and an Egyptian herald threatens war. In the (lost) next play in the trilogy, war is avoided when the girls agree to marriage, but they murder their husbands on their wedding night.

Aeschylus visited the court of Hiero, the tyrant of Syracuse, once or twice between his production of *Persians* in 472 and Hiero's death in 466. There he presented *Persians* and a new play, *Women of Aetna*, honoring Hiero's foundation of a city by the same name. *Myrmidons* may have established Aeschylus as a leading playwright in Athens, but *Persians* seems to have made him an international sensation.

Aeschylus must have presented other plays and won additional crowns as the decade of the 460s drew to a close, but we have no specific dates or titles until we arrive at the spring of 458. That was the year of his final Athenian production, the tragic trilogy called the *Oresteia*, which comprises *Agamemnon* and its sequels *Libation Bearers* and *Eumenides*. (Those plays are summarized in Appendix 1.[5])

The *Oresteia* won first place. In the wake of that triumph, Aeschylus returned to Sicily. He died there, under unknown circumstances, in the city of Gela, where he was buried.

The reader will have noticed that this account of Aeschylus' career omits a famous work, *Prometheus Bound*. Although that play was attributed to Aeschylus in antiquity, most scholars have been won over to the opinion that it was actually written by a later playwright. As Mark Griffith was the first to point out, *Prometheus Bound* has a number of stylistic features that are not found in Aeschylus' other six plays but are characteristic of later works by Sophocles and Euripides. The most obvious is the sharp decrease in the proportion of the play taken up by choral songs and chants in the anapestic meter. In Aeschylus' other six plays, an average of 42 percent of the lines are sung or chanted by the chorus. The lowest percentage (34 percent) occurs in *Eumenides*. In *Prometheus Bound*, the corresponding figure is 13 percent.[6] Such observations have led most scholars to describe the play's attribution to Aeschylus as doubtful at best. To account for the play's ancient attribution to him, Martin West has suggested that it was the work of Aeschylus' playwright son, Euphorion, presented posthumously as his father's.[7] The *Suda*'s entry for Euphorion says that he was a tragic poet in his own right but won four crowns presenting previously unproduced works by his father. Scholars have long found it hard to believe that Aeschylus left behind at his death the texts of sixteen unproduced plays. West has argued that Euphorion would have found it advantageous to present his own original work as his father's.

As mentioned above, ancient sources enlivened their generally reliable account of Aeschylus' career with suspect anecdotes. It is safe to assume, for example, that his invitations to the Syracusan court were tributes to his fame as a dramatist and that he was compensated for his trouble. His ancient biography, however, shares the report that he left Athens in dismay after being defeated by the young Sophocles,[8] while some of the *Suda*'s sources say it was because the stage in Athens collapsed during a performance of one of his plays. It was also said that the appearance of the chorus of Furies in his production of *Eumenides* caused pregnant women in the audience to miscarry.

The most famous of these dubious anecdotes concerns Aeschylus' death. An eagle, flying around with a turtle in its talons and looking for a way to break its shell open, saw the playwright's shiny bald head from the air. Mistaking it for a large rock, the eagle dropped the turtle, with results that were fatal for the poet.

Amid such fictions are at least two anecdotes that scholars take more seriously. First, it is widely reported that Aeschylus participated courageously in the great battles against the Persians that took place during his adulthood: Marathon (490), Salamis (480), and Plataea (479). Herodotus 6.114 states that Aeschylus' brother, Kynegeiros, died at Marathon. According to the story, Kynegeiros grabbed the stern ornament of a retreating Persian ship, and an enemy soldier chopped off his hand with an ax. I see no reason to doubt that Aeschylus lost a brother at Marathon, but the details of the death sound contrived to me.

Scholars seem most willing to accept another story that involves Marathon.[9] The ancient biography tells us that when

Aeschylus died in far-off Gela, the town's citizens buried him with great honors and erected a tombstone with this inscription:

> Here lies Aeschylus, Euphorion's son.
>> He died in grain-rich Gela.
> The grove of Marathon could speak of his valor,
>> as could the long-haired Mede, who knew it well.

The obviously fictional anecdotes about Aeschylus are disparaging and absurd. His supposed epitaph, on the other hand, is one of great dignity. For this reason, perhaps, a number of scholars are disposed to accept its authenticity and its implication that Aeschylus took greater pride in his achievements as a patriotic warrior than in his celebrated career as a poet. The story's implication that Aeschylus controlled the composition of his own epitaph gives one pause, but it is possible that he fell ill in Gela, sensed that his time was near, and dictated those words on his deathbed. The consensus seems to be that something like that actually happened.

Notes

1. E.g., *Inscriptiones Graecae*, vol. 2–3, part 2, 2318.

2. In the *Iliad* the Myrmidons are a Greek tribe commanded by Achilles.

3. A conclusion first defended by B. Döhle, "Die 'Achilleis' des Aischylos." For a more recent discussion with good photos, see Pantelis Michelakis, *Achilles in Greek Tragedy*, 31–36.

4. Fragment 135 probably contains the words of Achilles to Patroclus' corpse, rebuking him for the recklessness that led to his death: "You did not respect the sacred bond of our thighs. Poor thanks for those many kisses!" Alan H. Sommerstein, *Aeschylus, Fragments*, 144–145.

5. As usual, the production was actually a tetralogy. *Proteus*, the satyr play accompanying the tragedies, has not survived. It seems to have dealt with Menelaus' comical adventures when stranded in Egypt, as depicted in Book 4 of the *Odyssey*, where Proteus is an old shape-shifting merman whom Menelaus must wrestle into submission to learn how to get back home to Greece.

6. Mark Griffith, *The Authenticity of "Prometheus Bound,"* 123. The percentages are: *Persians*, 43; *Seven against Thebes*, 43; *Suppliants*, 55; *Agamemnon*, 41; *Libation Bearers*, 35; *Eumenides*, 34; *Prometheus*, 13. For Sophocles the average is 17 percent, with a high of 22.5 for *Antigone* and a low of 11 for *Electra*.

7. Martin L. West, *Studies in Aeschylus*, 70.

8. Plutarch (*Life of Cimon* 8.8–9) reports in addition that the contest between Aeschylus and the young Sophocles aroused such intense interest that the archon had the board of ten generals, including the great Cimon, judge the contest instead of selecting judges by chance, as was usually done. The story does not explain why Sophocles' first play aroused such interest.

9. See, e.g., Alan H. Sommerstein, s.v. Aeschylus, *Oxford Classical Dictionary*, 26.

Appendix 3

The *Oresteia* and Myth

Tantalus, a son of Zeus, was invited to a banquet of the gods.[1] To show how clever he could be, he killed his own son, Pelops, cut him into little pieces, and offered the child's flesh to the gods as his own contribution to the meal. Except for Demeter, the gods were not fooled.[2] They put Pelops' flesh into a cauldron and had one of the Fates, Clotho, work her magic. Pelops rose out of the cauldron as good as new—except that his shoulder was missing, eaten by the inattentive Demeter. The gods outfitted him with an ivory prosthesis. Poseidon, god of the sea, fell in love with the handsome youth and kept him on Mount Olympus as long as he remained young. Tantalus was punished for his crime by being imprisoned in the underworld with food and drink just out of reach and/or with a boulder teetering over his head.

When Pelops was grown, he was sent back to earth. At that time all the young men wanted to marry a maiden named Hippodamia. The catch was Hippodamia's father, Oenomaus, king of Pisa. An excellent charioteer, he decreed that Hippodamia would wed only a youth who could beat Oenomaus in a chariot race. Anyone who attempted to do so and failed would be killed. The road to his palace was littered with the skulls of failed suitors.

Citing their previous relationship, Pelops asked Poseidon for help in defeating Oenomaus. The god gave him a team of flying horses. Pelops won the race, married Hippodamia, and inherited the kingdom of Pisa, which included Olympia, the site of the original Olympic games. It is there that Pelops was buried.

Pelops' offspring included Atreus and Thyestes. According to Thucydides 1.9, Atreus was exiled on account of the death of his illegitimate half-brother, Chrysippus. We are left to infer that he had killed Chrysippus out of jealousy. Eurystheus, the king of Mycenae, was Atreus' nephew and entrusted the kingdom to his kinsman while Eurystheus made war on the children of his great enemy, Heracles—another story altogether. Eurystheus was killed in the course of that conflict, and Atreus settled down to rule Mycenae.

Thyestes apparently settled in Mycenae too. At the end of *Agamemnon*, Aegisthus recounts the rest of the story as it was apparently known to Aeschylus and his audience. According to Aegisthus, Thyestes challenged Atreus' power, but Atreus gained the upper hand and drove Thyestes into exile. Eventually, Thyestes appeared as a suppliant, asking to be allowed to come back home in safety. Atreus granted the request, swearing that Thyestes would not spill his blood in his fatherland. As a supposed gesture of hospitality, he invited Thyestes to a banquet. In preparation, he secretly killed and butchered two of Thyestes' three sons. Concealing their heads and limbs, he served their flesh to their father and then revealed his trick when Thyestes asked whether his sons could join the feast. Thyestes left, cursing Atreus and his entire family and taking with him his sole surviving son, Aegisthus, who was still an infant (*Agamemnon* 1583–1608). Aegisthus' account omits one detail to which Cassandra alludes: before going into exile, Thyestes had an affair with Atreus' wife (*Agamemnon* 1193).

Atreus died, leaving the kingdom of Mycenae to his eldest son, Agamemnon. Agamemnon's younger brother, Menelaus, married the beautiful Helen, queen of Sparta, while Agamemnon married Helen's sister, Clytaemestra. Hence each brother, each Atreid, possessed a throne: Agamemnon, Mycenae's; Menelaus, Sparta's. (Aeschylus took the liberty of referring to Agamemnon's kingdom as the nearby city of Argos.[3]) As is well known, all of Helen's many suitors had sworn to defend her and her chosen husband, whoever that turned out to be.[4] In time, Menelaus and Helen received a visitor, Paris, the charming prince of Troy. When Menelaus was required to leave the city because of some urgent business in Crete, Helen ran away with Paris. She was not abducted but left of her own free will— unless the goddess Aphrodite made her do it.[5]

The result was the Trojan War. Although Menelaus was the aggrieved husband, Agamemnon became the expedition's supreme commander. Greek kings, warlords in our terms, gathered with their forces at the seaside town of Aulis, preparing to sail to Troy. Before the fleet departed, Agamemnon angered the huntress goddess Artemis by killing a deer and boasting that he was as good a hunter as she. His priest informed him that before his army could conquer Troy, he would have to sacrifice his daughter, Iphigenia, on Artemis' altar to pay for his boastfulness. Agamemnon complied. Artemis, however, rescued Iphigenia at the last moment, replacing her with a deer and spiriting her away to a temple on the shores of the Black Sea.[6]

Agamemnon then led the Greek fleet to Troy. Years passed. In Mycenae, Aegisthus arrived at the palace and succeeded in winning Clytaemestra's heart.[7] They lived together and laid plans to murder Agamemnon upon his return. In the earliest extant version of this story, Homer's, they are motivated by lust. Around the same time as the production of the *Oresteia*, the poet Pindar raised the question of whether Clytaemestra was motivated instead by the desire to gain revenge for the sacrifice of Iphigenia (*Pythian* 11.17–21). In Aeschylus' version, she claims to be seeking justice. By the same token, Aegisthus says that he is only after revenge for the crime against Thyestes.

Ten years after their arrival on Trojan shores, the Greek army succeeded in storming Troy, thanks to the wooden horse trick. Various stories are told about the Greeks' barbarity in victory. Ajax the Lesser, for example, raped Cassandra, daughter of the king of Troy and priestess of Apollo, in Athena's temple as she clung to the goddess's statue.[8] Such acts incurred the hostility of the gods. As a result, the Greeks generally had a difficult time getting home or ran into trouble when they got there.

Aeschylus' *Agamemnon* is set in Mycenae, renamed Argos, beginning on the very night that Troy fell.

Notes

1. Pindar's *Olympian* 1.30–87 is the earliest source for the story of Tantalus and Pelops, from Tantalus' offense through Pelops' marriage. Pindar claims that some of the details are impious lies, but he takes obvious pleasure in repeating them.

2. The role of Demeter (Roman Ceres) is preserved in Hyginus, *Fabula* 83.

3. Mycenae had fallen on hard times by Aeschylus' time. In the 460s it was destroyed by its neighbor Argos, which did not want another state encroaching on its territory. Around the same time, Athens abandoned an alliance with Sparta and joined forces with Sparta's rival, Argos (Thucydides 1.102.4). Aeschylus refrains from mentioning that Menelaus and Helen had been king and queen of Sparta.

4. The earliest source for the suitors' oath appears to be Hesiod's *Catalogue of Women* (Fragment 155 Most; 204 West), which says that Menelaus was selected because he offered the most gifts.

5. This part of the story was found in the *Cypria*, an archaic Greek poem on the beginnings of the Trojan War. It is preserved only in the form of a brief summary by the fifth-century CE scholar Proclus.

6. This is the version found in the *Cypria*.

7. Aegisthus' seduction of Clytaemestra is described in *Odyssey* 1.35–43 and 3.262–275.

8. A description of this event appears in the fragments of the sixth-century BCE poet Alcaeus: D. L. Page, *Supplementum Lyricis Graecis*, 262. Ajax the Lesser died at sea with an assist from Poseidon (*Odyssey* 4.499–511).

Appendix 4

The *Oresteia* and Politics

Two important and reliable sources of information about Athenian politics around the time the *Oresteia* was first presented survive: a passage in Thucydides' history called the *pentecontaetia* ("the fifty years") and a few sentences in an essay by Aristotle, the *Constitution of the Athenians*. These sources focus on two separate events, both occurring shortly before the premier of the *Oresteia* and constituting pivotal points in the evolution of the Athenian state. Aeschylus' trilogy alludes to both events in ways that point to definite conclusions about his politics.

After the Persian Wars, Athens had quickly developed into an imperial power. It maintained a battle-ready fleet with the ostensible purpose of protecting Greek city-states in the Aegean and on the coast of Turkey from further Persian attacks, and it collected tribute from them in return for this protection. Attempts by resentful "allies" to secede from the empire were brutally repressed. Meanwhile, thousands of Athenians made their livings by tending to one of the many tasks involved in running the empire (Aristotle, *Constitution of the Athenians* 24).

The only Greek state strong enough to rival Athens was Sparta. The two had cooperated in repelling the Persians. Since Athens was a naval power and Sparta a land power, there was reason to hope that they would prolong their mutually beneficial relationship indefinitely. In each state, however, factions emerged that were distrustful of the other.

The Spartans were especially distrustful. Not only was Athens' empire constantly growing, but it had recently adopted a democratic constitution under which the greatest power was in the hands of the assembly of all male citizens. This meant that their politics was dominated by "common men," the large number of citizens at the bottom of the economic ladder—the *demos* in Aristotle's terms.

Such a system was anathema to Sparta, Greece's oldest oligarchy, which was in fact viewed as a model of good government by traditionalists, including some of Athens' wealthy aristocrats. The leader of the aristocratic, pro-Spartan faction in Athens was Cimon, a general. The commander of Athens' fleet since the end of the Persian Wars, he had expanded the Athenian empire with several successful engagements in the Aegean and even ventured into the eastern Mediterranean to destroy a Persian fleet at the battle of Eurymedon in 466 BCE (Thucydides 1.98.1–3, 1.100.1). As long as Cimon's successes continued, the party of the people had little grounds for challenging the leadership of the aristocrats.

The pivotal event reported by Thucydides grew out of a situation in Sparta. It had conquered the southwestern Peloponnesus in the so-called Messenian Wars, a series of poorly documented conflicts that played out in the seventh century. The conquered Messenians were reduced to the status of serfs ("helots"). Around 463 the helots revolted and took refuge in a fortified mountain. The Spartans laid siege to them but were unable to storm the mountain fortress and sought assistance from their allies, including Athens. Cimon was happy to oblige and led some four thousand hoplites to the spot. When the Athenians failed to turn the tide, the Spartans began to suspect that they secretly favored the helots. As a result, they sent the

Athenians home without an explanation. The Athenian reaction was extreme. Feeling insulted, they renounced their treaty with Sparta and concluded one with Sparta's major rival in the Peloponnesus, Argos (Thucydides 1.102).

Alert readers of Homer are surprised when they turn to the *Oresteia* and find Agamemnon and Orestes described as kings of Argos rather than kings of Mycenae, as Homer would have it. It is equally odd that Menelaus' homeland, traditionally Sparta, is never mentioned at all. Politics accounts for these peculiarities. This is obvious from Orestes' final speech in *Eumenides* (754–777), where he thanks Athena for restoring him to his Argive homeland and promises the people of Athens that no Argive army will ever invade their land. Even after he dies, his ghost will make sure that any invasion will fail miserably. This celebration of the Argos alliance strongly suggests that Aeschylus' sympathies lay with the anti-Spartan party of the people, for whom the shift was a major victory.

The Areopagus Council was at the heart of the pivotal event described by Aristotle. The Areopagus itself is a rocky plateau next to the Acropolis. The council that met there consisted of former high-ranking magistrates ("archons") drawn from the top two of the four property classes. In earlier times the Areopagus Council was the state's highest authority. Judging by Aristotle's description, it operated like a proactive supreme court—one with conservative tendencies: "The Council of Areopagites had the job of guarding the laws, and it managed most of the most important affairs in the city, punishing and fining all those in authority who acted improperly. The selection of archons was based on merit and wealth, and the Areopagites were chosen from them" (*Constitution of the Athenians* 3.6). Aristotle goes on to say that the Areopagus Council's power and prestige were enhanced by its good management of affairs during the Persian Wars and that it continued to exercise its traditional role smoothly for seventeen years thereafter—that is, until 462.

At that time the champion of the demos was a man named Ephialtes. He orchestrated an attack on the Areopagus Council and succeeded in transferring its powers to more democratic institutions: "First he removed many of the Areopagites by bringing suits against them concerning their management of affairs. Then, during the archonship of Conon [462/461 BCE], he stripped the council of all the added functions through which it was the guardian of the law. Some of these he assigned to the Council of 500, others to the demos and its juries"[1] (*Constitution of the Athenians* 25.2–3). No longer the guardian of the laws in general, the Areopagus was reduced to hearing cases of intentional homicide and little else of significance.

Aeschylus' *Eumenides* depicts the foundation of the Areopagus Council by Athena in an entirely positive light. One's first impression is that he must have been critical of attacks against it such as Ephialtes', but some words that he puts into Athena's mouth complicate the picture. In supposedly founding the council, she says that the citizens' regard for it will always combat injustice, provided that they do not change the laws, like people who add mud and filth to clean water (*Eumenides* 690–695). Athena's words obviously allude to some supposedly misguided extension of the Areopagus' authority. They cannot refer directly to Ephialtes' reforms, which reduced the council's powers. In the context of the time, I think that these words must be read as justification for Ephialtes' reforms. He and his supporters could have justified changes in the ancient institution only by arguing that the powers his legislation eliminated were late, muddy additions to the pure water of the council's original charter.

Aeschylus' depiction of the Furies is consistent with the Areopagus' severely restricted function. Early on, they describe their fated role as follows:

> *Since birth it's been established*
> *we haven't any right*

> *to touch divinities*
> *or share an acolyte,*
> *—or go to holy feasts*
> *in robes of lily white.*
>
> *We choose to level houses*
> *reveling in sin,*
> *when Ares turns domestic*
> *and someone murders kin.*
> *However powerful*
> *that person may have been,*
> *we chase and apprehend him*
> *and drain the blood within.*
>
> (347–359)

During their reconciliation with Athena, the Furies seem capable of delivering healthy crops and herds and happy family lives, but there is no indication that their judicial powers extend beyond crimes against blood relatives. In earlier times, the Athenians divided themselves into four tribes based on ancestry. A central feature of the new democracy was the redistribution of the population into ten new tribes based on place of residence, not blood. By emphatically associating the Furies with crimes against blood relatives, Aeschylus seems to relegate them to concerns of the past and thereby to endorse Ephialtes' reforms.

Those reforms were deeply resented in some quarters. Aristotle mentions in passing that Ephialtes was assassinated soon after their adoption. Historians have some doubts, since the murder, if it happened, ought to have inspired more comment. In one way or another, however, Ephialtes passed from the scene, leaving the party of the people in a much stronger position. Its new leader was Pericles.

If my understanding of the *Oresteia* is correct, Aeschylus used his artistry in part to support the policies of the demos. This bias seems enlightened in the sense that it was a step in the direction of government "by the people." On the other hand, the guidance of the Athenian state by the demos left a lot to be desired. The acquisition of an empire had made Athens wealthy. The demos shared in the wealth and was greedy for more. Constant warfare was the result. Around the time of the *Oresteia*'s premier, the Athenians sent a fleet of two hundred ships and a later relief force of sixty ships to Egypt to aid the Egyptians' attempt to gain their independence from Persia. Both fleets were eventually lost. In the quarter-century that followed, the Athenians subjugated the island of Aegina, extinguished revolts in Euboea, Samos, and Byzantium, briefly conquered Boeotia, seized control of Delphi and handed it over to their allies from Phocis, and defeated the Persians in Cyprus—among other actions (Thucydides 1.104–117).

Aeschylus' Athena endorses that kind of militaristic hyperactivity. After asking the Furies not to plant a love of civil strife in the hearts of Athenians, she adds:

> Let foreign wars rage on, enough to sate
> the man who knows the urgent love of fame!
> (864–865)

These activities increasingly alarmed Sparta and its allies, who felt with some justification that the Athenians would not be satisfied until they had subjugated the entire Greek world. The eventual result was the Peloponnesian War of 431–404 BCE, a twenty-seven-year conflict that pitted Sparta and its allies against Athens, brought widespread misery to the Greek world, and finally resulted in Athens' humiliating surrender.

Note

1. The Council of 500 was established in 508/507 BCE to prepare the docket for meetings of the Assembly. It was more democratic than the Areopagus Council in that it was open to the top three property classes and its

membership consisted of fifty individuals from each of the ten new tribes founded by Cleisthenes on the basis of place of residence rather than ancestry (unlike the four original kinship-based tribes). The demos, the common people, exercised their power through meetings of the Assembly, in which all adult male citizens could participate, and through trials referred to them and adjudicated by jurors chosen by lot from six thousand volunteers.

Appendix 5

Renaming *Eumenides*

In 1984 the classicist A. L. Brown gathered evidence that the traditional title of the *Oresteia*'s third play, *Eumenides*, was a mistake based on slipshod ancient scholarship.[1] In 1996 this conclusion was endorsed and amplified by Alan H. Sommerstein, the editor and translator of the Loeb Library Aeschylus.[2] The rejection of the traditional title cleared the way for a much better understanding of what the play meant to Aeschylus' original audience and what it means to us.

Three names for groups of mysterious chthonic goddesses are involved. First in mythological time come the Erinyes, appalling, snake-haired[3] females who appear (though only to Orestes) at the end of *Libation Bearers*. They also constitute the chorus in the play traditionally called *Eumenides*. In it they wear filthy black rags and headdresses that look like tangled snakes. The etymology of "Erinyes" is uncertain. Pausanias (8.25.6) derives it from a dialectal verb for being angry: hence, the "Angry Ones" or the Latinate "Furies."

According to Hesiod, in *Theogony* 183–185, the Furies were born from the drops of blood that fell to earth when Cronus castrated his father, Uranus (Heaven). Their main function in myth suits their birth from the primordial attack of a son on a father: they are vengeful spirits who punish children who commit sins against their parents. Orestes, the matricide, qualified easily. The Furies also go after perjurers. To explain that proclivity, Hesiod tells us that they were the midwives at the birth of Oath (*Works and Days* 803–804). In the *Iliad*, they stop a horse from speaking (19.259–260). Elsewhere Heraclitus (Fragment 94) adds that as helpers of Justice they keep the sun on course. The last two functions reflect the ancient Greek tendency to lump moral law and natural law together. The eventual punishment of those who sin against their parents was thought to be as certain as the sun rising in the east or horses not speaking. Both kinds of law were enforced by the Furies. They had no home base; they could appear anywhere in the mythological world where their services were needed.

Unlike the Furies, the second group was a purely Athenian institution with a specific location: a fissure in the earth at the foot of the Hill of Ares or "Areopagus," a rocky plateau on the northwestern side of the Acropolis.[4] This fissure was believed to be an entrance to the underworld occupied by mysterious female deities known only as "the Holy Goddesses" (*hai Semnai Theai*). Nearby stood altars where Athenians and foreigners offered sacrifices to the goddesses. The Assembly even passed resolutions asking the goddesses for favors for the state.

Anyone touching the altars was under the goddesses' protection. To kill such a suppliant for any reason was a serious sin. The person responsible and all of his descendants were cursed and therefore unfit to participate in any communal activity. In the 600s BCE participants in a failed attempt to establish a tyranny in Athens were dragged away from the goddesses' altars and killed. The magistrate responsible was a member of the distinguished Alcmeonid clan. For centuries their enemies brought up the goddesses' curse and demanded the banishment of prominent members of the clan, including Cleisthenes, the legislative founder of democracy, in 510 BCE, and Pericles, Athens' leading statesman and general, in 432.[5]

The Areopagus was the meeting place of the powerful Areopagus Council (see Appendix 4). Dinarchus (1.47) mentions that the Holy Goddesses were invoked in oaths taken at the homicide cases tried on the Areopagus.

Unlike "Erinyes," "Holy Goddesses" is not a true proper name. It could be applied to any group of female deities. Such generic titles bring with them the possibility that some more distinctive name is being held in reserve. Such is the case with the Holy Goddesses, who were worshipped in Athens for centuries, during which no one seemed to know a more specific name for them. The mystery of their identity must have enhanced their aura.

For the finale of the *Oresteia*, Aeschylus invented the myth that these mysterious goddesses were actually the Furies, Hesiod's terrifying goddesses who dwelt in the underworld and punished sinners, the spirits of vengeance who haunted the Greek world of myth and legend. The moment of revelation comes at line 1041 when the chorus of Athena's acolytes addresses the Furies as *Semnai Theai*[6] while preparing to escort them to their new underground chambers, an apparent reference to the aforementioned fissure in the earth. No Athenian would doubt that those words signaled the identification of the Furies with the Holy Goddesses. The Furies, however, had undergone a change, transformed by their interaction with Athena and the Athenians during and after Orestes' trial. Early in the play (line 125), the ghost of Clytaemestra asks the sleeping Furies rhetorically if causing harm isn't their only function. At that point in the story it is, but Athena's generosity awakens in them the power also to do good by promoting agriculture and civic peace. The identification of the two groups of gods also enhances the status of the Holy Goddesses. In their negative aspects, like the punishment of perjury, they are worthy of profound fear. No longer just the gods of a local cult, they are cosmic forces. Sommerstein writes, "When Aeschylus identified the *Semnai*

Theai of Athens with the Erinyes who had pursued Orestes, he was making a startling innovation which, if his audience accepted it, would revolutionize their understanding of the significance of both groups of deities."[7]

How then did the third group, the Eumenides, become involved? Their name is derived from an adjective meaning "gracious," but it is a proper name and therefore usually left untranslated. There is evidence that there were cults of the Eumenides in a few places in the Greek world in the early fifth century, but not in Athens.[8] Like the Erinyes and the *Semnai*, the Eumenides were chthonic powers who were responsible for blessings as well as curses. In art they were pictured holding snakes in one hand and flowers in the other—apparently to symbolize their dual nature. Eumenides are not mentioned by name in *Eumenides* or in any work of Greek literature until the appearance of Euripides' *Orestes* in 408 BCE. In that play the goddesses chasing Orestes are called "Eumenides" four time and "Erinyes" three. It is clear that "Eumenides" has become an alternative term for "Erinyes," and this usage was common from then on. The motive for adopting an alternative name was probably the desire to avoid ill-omened words, as "Erinyes" was felt to be: the "Angry Ones" were referred to euphemistically—or perhaps ironically—as the "Gracious Ones." The inspiration for this usage must have been a work of literature, subsequently lost, in which the name change figured prominently. As Brown points out, just such a work is referenced in the scholia to Sophocles' *Oedipus at Colonus* at line 42: "Some say that [the Furies] changed their name in dealing with Orestes; for they were first called Eumenides when they became gracious towards him after he prevailed in his trial before the Athenians and sacrificed a black sow to the Furies in the Peloponnesian Ceryneia."[9] It seems that this story or one like it established the usage. Under its influence, Aeschylus' play, which may have originally been called *Erinyes*, was changed for the sake of propriety to *Eumenides*. Ancient scholars who composed summaries of plays then assumed falsely that this name change was dramatized in the play. The play's hypothesis in the best manuscripts reads in part: "Surrounded by the Furies in Delphi, Orestes went, on the advice of Apollo, to the temple of Athena. Having prevailed with her advice, he returned to Argos. Having calmed the Furies, he addressed them as 'Eumenides.'" In fact, in the text as we have it, Orestes leaves Athens for Argos without addressing the Furies.

Efforts have been made to salvage this summary. Some have argued that the name change to "Eumenides" must have occurred in a passage that was omitted by scribal error, but this hardly seems defensible. If Aeschylus introduced the idea of calling the Furies "Eumenides" in 458, why did the usage suddenly become popular fifty years later? Besides, the surviving text of *Eumenides* does depict a bold name change—when Athena's chorus addresses the Furies as the *Semnai Theai*. One such change is enough. The time has come to rename the play. I like *The Holy Goddesses*.

Notes

1. A. L. Brown, "Eumenides in Greek Tragedy."
2. Alan H. Sommerstein, *Aeschylean Tragedy*, 204.
3. See *Libation Bearers* 1048–1050, mentioned in Pausanias 1.28.6.
4. J. G. Frazer vouches for the existence of such a fissure in his commentary on Pausanias: *Pausanias's Description of Greece*, vol. 2: *Commentary on Book 1*, 366–367. I have not seen it.
5. The main sources for the *Semnai*'s cult are Thucydides 126.2–12, Pausanias 1.28.6, and Plutarch, *Solon* 12. For a complete list see Brown, "Eumenides in Greek Tragedy," 262.
6. Only the word "Semnai" occurs in the manuscript. Editors generally restore "Theai," on the assumption that it was omitted by scribal error. The phrase "Semnai Theai" is common and fits the meter.
7. Sommerstein, *Aeschylean Tragedy*, 204.

8. The grove sacred to the Eumenides in *Oedipus at Colonus* seems fictitious, since it borrows well-known features from the Areopagus and the *Semnai*'s precinct. See the introduction to my translation of Sophocles' *Oedipus at Colonus* (xliii–xlv).

9. Quoted and translated in Brown, "Eumenides in Greek Tragedy," 271. For the complete Greek text, see Page, *Aeschyli, Septem quae supersunt tragoedias*, 246. Ceryneia was a small city on the south coast of the Corinthian Gulf. Pausanias 7.25.7 states that there was a sanctuary of the Eumenides there, founded by Orestes.

Appendix 6

Metrical Terms and Practices

Rhythm in speech is created—as it is in a beating heart—by high points of exertion occurring at regular intervals. Meters are linguistic patterns that lend themselves to being pronounced rhythmically. Whereas English poetry depends on patterns of stressed and unstressed syllables, ancient Greek meters consist of patterns of long and short syllables. Nevertheless the same terminology is applied to poetry in both languages and similar patterns occur. An unstressed (or short) syllable followed by a stressed (or long) is an iamb (short/long). The reverse, a stressed syllable followed by an unstressed, is a trochee (long/short). Two stressed syllables make a spondee (long/long). Two unstressed syllables followed by a stressed one make an anapest (short/short/long) and a stressed syllable followed by two unstressed ones make a dactyl (long/short/short).

Most speech in the *Oresteia* and other ancient Greek tragedies consists of lines called iambic trimeters: three pairs of feet in which an iamb or a spondee is followed by a mandatory iamb. I translate these into iambic pentameters in English: lines of five iambs. For example, "*Omoi!* I'm struck a fatal blow within!" (1343) For variety, I allow trochees in the first foot and spondees everywhere.

Instead of iambs, *Agamemnon* ends with a spoken passage containing lines of four pairs of trochees with a syllable missing at the very end (a meter known as "trochaic tetrameter catalectic"). Trochaic lines read more rapidly than iambics and lend themselves to the representation of excited speech; for example, "Exiles eagerly devour empty hopes. How well I know!" (1668).

The other meter often used in tragedy and not meant to be sung is the anapestic dipody: two pairs of anapests in which spondees and dactyls are allowed. Strings of anapestic dipodies are used in chants, sometimes preludes to choral songs. They were not sung but recited with an emphatic, repetitious rhythm as though by marching soldiers. In fact, anapests are used by the chorus of *Agamemnon* when it first marches onto the scene. My imitation anapestic lines consist of three or four anapests, with the first one normally reduced to a single stressed syllable, a spondee, or an iamb; for example, "The words of antiquity ring in our ears: / the doer must suffer the deed" (*Libation Bearers* 312–313).

Since we lack the critical knowledge of the melodies involved, I have not attempted to imitate the complicated meters used in passages meant to be sung. Instead I translate those passages (which are italicized in my text) into short rhymed stanzas so that they sound like songs to English-speaking readers.

The longer choral songs are divided into pairs of metrical paragraphs or stanzas known as *strophes* and *antistrophes* (turnings and returnings). The metrical pattern introduced by any given strophe had to be reproduced, syllable for syllable, by its corresponding antistrophe. In my translation, antistrophes have the same number of lines and patterns of end rhyme as their corresponding strophes. For example:

> *The thoughts men have are grandiose*
> *so long as skies are bright.*

They wilt, however, underground,
and all their pride takes flight
when they behold our angry dance
and robes as dark as night.

(Strophe *Eumenides* 367–371)

The fallen man does not know why.
His mind is quite undone.
Such is the dark, polluted cloud
that hovers over one.
Sad rumors say that round his house
a fog obscures the sun.

(Antistrophe *Eumenides* 377–380)

The other constituents of Aeschylus' choral songs are mesodes, musical passages inserted between a strophe and antistrophe; epodes, musical passages coming at the end of strophic pairs; and epirrhemata (singular: epirrhema), spoken comments taking the place of mesodes or epodes.

The best example of the elaborate structures sometimes built from those units is the song sung by Cassandra in *Agamemnon* (1072–1177). The song contains seven strophic pairs—fourteen lyrical outbursts. Cassandra's strophes and antistrophes grow steadily longer. In the first four instances, the coryphaeus offers a spoken two-line comment, an epirhema, after each strophe and each antistrophe. In the fifth movement (1114–1135), there is a spike in the hymn's complexity. Each of the epirrhemata is followed by four lyrical lines sung by the chorus, hence: strophe, epirrhema, mesode, antistrophe, epirrhema, epode.

CASSANDRA:
Oh keep the cow and bull apart,
lest otherwise, be warned!
She'll trap the bull in woven robes.
She takes her hidden horn.

She strikes. He falls where waters wash
his wounded body clean,
a basin built for taking baths,
a clever death machine.

CORYPHAEUS:
I never could interpret oracles,
but that sounds rather ominous to me.

CHORUS:
What good has ever come of these
verbose, ill-sounding prophecies?
They only rob our hearts of ease
by teaching us new fear.

(*Agamemnon* 1125–1135)

In the sixth movement (1136–1155), the coryphaeus is silent. Cassandra's strophic pair evokes sung comments, a mesode and an epode, from the chorus. The finale (1156–1177), repeats the pattern of the fifth movement except that Cassandra herself provides the epirrhemata; that is, she comments on her strophe and antistrophe in a speaking voice herself.

The lamentation of Orestes and Electra at their father's grave (*Libation Bearers* 315–475) has an even more remarkable structure. The chorus takes turns with Electra and Orestes in singing. In my schema (below) each number stands in its first occurrence for a strophe and in its second for the corresponding antistrophe. "An" stands for an anapestic interlude where singing gives way to chanting. Hence the song consists of eleven interwoven strophic pairs punctuated by chants at several points.

1-2-1 / An / 3-2-3 / An / 4-5-4 / An / 6-5-6 / 7-8-9 / 9-7-8 /10-10 / 11-11

I was not able to adhere to a line-by-line translation of anapestic chants or lyrical passages. In those cases marginal line numbers indicate the portion of the Greek text covered by each passage, not the slightly different number of lines in my translation. For example, my marginal note indicates that the opening anapestic march in *Agamemnon* takes up lines 40 through 103 in the Greek text. I omit the information that it covers lines 40 through 107 in my translation.

Appendix 7

The Greek Stage

In picturing Greek tragedies, one should keep it in mind that all the participants were male. The cast consisted of a chorus and speaking actors. In the period of the *Oresteia,* there were three speaking actors and twelve members of the chorus. Everyone wore masks. That enabled the actors to play different roles by changing masks offstage. In *Agamemnon,* for example, the same actor would probably play both the watchman on the palace roof and the herald who brings news of Agamemnon's return.

The chorus' function was to sing and dance to musical accompaniment. The leader of the chorus or "coryphaeus" also engaged in spoken exchanges with the actors. Occasionally, actors were also required to sing. In *Agamemnon,* the role of Cassandra calls for an excellent singer.

Greek theaters were constructed on hillsides and consisted of four essential parts, besides the audience seated on the hill. The *skēnē,* or stage building at the foot of the hill, provided the backdrop to the action. It was painted to represent an entrance of some kind, a royal residence, a temple, a soldier's hut, whatever the story called for. Actors often entered or exited through its doors. The unseen interior of the skēnē was used as a changing room.

The area that we call a stage was the *proskēnion*, literally what lies in front of the skēnē. A round or rectangular *orchēstra*, or dancing place, lay in front of the proskēnion. There members of the chorus sang and danced during the frequent musical interludes.

Finally, a *parodos* (plural, *parodoi*), or passageway, ran along either side of the proskēnion, starting from behind the skēnē and ending in the orchēstra. Choruses typically made their first entrance via a parodos. Songs that choruses sang while entering and speeches addressed directly to the audience in comedies were also called parodoi.

Most of the entrances and exits in the *Oresteia* are made via parodoi. The players may have observed a distinction between parodoi: one associated with nearby destinations, the other with more remote ones. Thus in *Agamemnon*, which is set before the royal residence, the chorus would enter via the local parodos because the choristers come from the city itself; the herald and Agamemnon and Cassandra would enter via the other because they were coming from far-away Troy.

Exits and entrances in and out of the skēnē are also frequent and require little comment. A special effect associated with the skēnē is the *ekkekulēma*, or roller. This was a wooden trolley that could be rolled out through the skēnē's open doors. It supported tableaus representing situations inside the skēnē. It is not known whether the ekkekulēma was used in Aeschylus' day. However, there are three scenes in the *Oresteia* that may have been written with it in mind: in *Agamemnon*, Clytaemestra vaunting over the bodies of Agamemnon and Cassandra (after line 1371); in *Libation Bearers*, Orestes standing over the bodies of his mother and Aegisthus (after line 971); and in *Eumenides*, the appearance of Orestes praying to Apollo inside his temple (after line 63).

The most famous of special effects, the *mēchanē* or machine, may not yet have been in use in Aeschylus' day either. It was a kind of crane that enabled actors to make airborne entrances and exits. The possible occasions that I see for its use in the *Oresteia* are Apollo's sudden arrival (lines 574–575) and unnoticed departure in the Athenian portion of *Eumenides*. Concerning Apollo's departure, we have only his remark (line 677) that he will stay to hear the verdict. In fact, nothing is heard from him once Athena announces that Orestes is acquitted (line 752). That is the moment at which he must have made exit.

The abruptness of Apollo's entrance and exit may be accounted for by defects in the manuscript, but I am inclined to think that it is dramatically appropriate and deliberate. The fact that no one comments on Apollo's approach or departure can be accounted for by their suddenness: he came and went too quickly for anyone to say anything. Perhaps, he just dropped from the sky, then flew off like a bird. There may also be an allusion to Apollo's flight earlier in the text. At line 404 Athena, entering via a parodos, mentions that she made her way from Troy on foot without the use of wings. That seems to imply that an airborne arrival was possible.

Bibliography

Brown, A. L. "Eumenides in Greek Tragedy." *Classical Quarterly* 34 (1984): 260–81.

Döhle, B. "Die 'Achilleis' des Aischylos in ihrer Auswirkung auf die attische Vasenmalerei des 5. Jahrhunderts." *Klio* 49 (1967): 63–149.

Fraenkel, Eduard, ed. *Aeschylus: "Agamemnon."* 3 vols. Edited with a commentary. Oxford: Clarendon Press, 1950.

Frazer, J. G. *Pausanias's Description of Greece*, vol. 2: *Commentary on Book 1*. New York: Biblo and Tannen, 1965.

Gantz, Timothy. *Early Greek Myth: A Guide to Literary and Artistic Sources*. 2 vols. Baltimore: Johns Hopkins University Press, 1993.

Garvie, A. F. *Aeschylus: "Choephori."* New York: Oxford University Press, 1986.

Griffith, Mark. *The Authenticity of "Prometheus Bound."* Cambridge: Cambridge University Press, 1977.

Michelakis, Pantelis. *Achilles in Greek Tragedy*. Cambridge: Cambridge University Press, 2002.

Page, D. L. *Aeschyli, Septem quae supersunt tragoedias*. Oxford: Oxford University Press, 1972.

———. *Supplementum Lyricis Graecis*. Oxford: Oxford University Press, 1974.

Podlecki, A. J. *Aeschylus: "Eumenides."* Warminster: Aris & Phillips, 1989.

Raeburn, David, and Oliver Thomas. *The "Agamemnon" of Aeschylus: A Commentary for Students*. Oxford: Oxford University Press, 2011.

Sommerstein, Alan H. *Aeschylean Tragedy*. Bari: Levante Editori, 1996.

———. "Aeschylus." In *Oxford Classical Dictionary*. Oxford: Oxford University Press, 2012.

———. *Aeschylus, Eumenides.* Cambridge: Cambridge University Press, 1989.

———. *Aeschylus, Fragments.* Cambridge, MA: Harvard University Press, 2008.

———. *Aeschylus, "Oresteia": "Agamemnon," "Libation-Bearers," "Eumenides."* Cambridge, MA: Harvard University Press, 2008.

———. "Comic Elements in Tragic Language: The Case of Aeschylus." In *The Language of Greek Comedy*, edited by A. Willi, 154–56. Oxford: Oxford University Press, 2002.

Sophocles. *Oedipus at Colonus.* Translated by David Mulroy. Madison: University of Wisconsin Press, 2014.

Taplin, Oliver. *The Stagecraft of Aeschylus: The Dramatic Use of Exits and Entrances in Greek Tragedy.* Oxford: Oxford University Press, 1977.

West, Martin L. *Studies in Aeschylus.* Stuttgart: B.G. Teubner, 1990.

WISCONSIN STUDIES IN CLASSICS

Patricia A. Rosenmeyer, Laura McClure,
Mark Stansbury-O'Donnell, and Matthew Roller

Series Editors

Romans and Barbarians: The Decline of the Western Empire
E. A. Thompson

A History of Education in Antiquity
H. I. Marrou
Translated from the French by George Lamb

Accountability in Athenian Government
Jennifer Tolbert Roberts

Festivals of Attica: An Archaeological Commentary
Erika Simon

Roman Cities: Les villes romaines
Pierre Grimal
Edited and translated by G. Michael Woloch

Ancient Greek Art and Iconography
Edited by Warren G. Moon

Kallimachos: The Alexandrian Library and the Origins of Bibliography
Rudolf Blum
Translated by Hans H. Wellisch

Myth, Ethos, and Actuality: Official Art in Fifth Century B.C. Athens
David Castriota

Archaic Greek Poetry: An Anthology
Selected and translated by Barbara Hughes Fowler

Murlo and the Etruscans: Art and Society in Ancient Etruria
Edited by Richard Daniel De Puma and Jocelyn Penny Small

The Wedding in Ancient Athens
John H. Oakley and Rebecca H. Sinos

The World of Roman Costume
Edited by Judith Lynn Sebesta and Larissa Bonfante

Greek Heroine Cults
Jennifer Larson

Flinders Petrie: A Life in Archaeology
Margaret S. Drower

Polykleitos, the Doryphoros, and Tradition
Edited by Warren G. Moon

The Game of Death in Ancient Rome: Arena Sport and Political Suicide
Paul Plass

Polygnotos and Vase Painting in Classical Athens
Susan B. Matheson

Worshipping Athena: Panathenaia and Parthenon
Edited by Jenifer Neils

Modes of Viewing in Hellenistic Poetry and Art
Graham Zanker

Religion in Ancient Etruria
Jean-René Jannot
Translated by Jane K. Whitehead

A Symposion of Praise: Horace Returns to Lyric in "Odes" IV
Timothy Johnson

Satire and the Threat of Speech: Horace's "Satires," Book 1
Catherine M. Schlegel

Prostitutes and Courtesans in the Ancient World
Edited by Christopher A. Faraone and Laura K. McClure

Asinaria: The One about the Asses
Plautus
Translated and with commentary by John Henderson

Ulysses in Black: Ralph Ellison, Classicism, and African American Literature
Patrice D. Rankine

Imperium and Cosmos: Augustus and the Northern Campus Martius
Paul Rehak
Edited by John G. Younger

Ovid before Exile: Art and Punishment in the "Metamorphoses"
Patricia J. Johnson

Pandora's Senses: The Feminine Character of the Ancient Text
Vered Lev Kenaan

Nox Philologiae: Aulus Gellius and the Fantasy of the Roman Library
Erik Gunderson

Antigone
Sophocles
A verse translation by David Mulroy, with introduction and notes

Aeschylus's "Suppliant Women": The Tragedy of Immigration
Geoffrey W. Bakewell

Couched in Death: "Klinai" and Identity in Anatolia and Beyond
Elizabeth P. Baughan

Silence in Catullus
Benjamin Eldon Stevens

Odes
Horace
Translated with commentary by David R. Slavitt

Shaping Ceremony: Monumental Steps and Greek Architecture
Mary B. Hollinshead

Selected Epigrams
Martial
Translated with notes by Susan McLean

The Offense of Love: "Ars Amatoria," "Remedia Amoris," and "Tristia" 2
Ovid
A verse translation by Julia Dyson Hejduk, with introduction and notes

Oedipus at Colonus
Sophocles
A verse translation by David Mulroy, with introduction and notes

Women in Roman Republican Drama
Edited by Dorota Dutsch, Sharon L. James, and David Konstan

Dream, Fantasy, and Visual Art in Roman Elegy
Emma Scioli

Printed in the United States
By Bookmasters